CROSSCURRENTS
PURSUING SOCIAL JUSTICE AND INTERRELIGIOUS WORK
SINCE 1950

CrossCurrents (ISSN 0011-1953; online ISSN 1939-3881) connects the wisdom of the heart with the life of the mind and the experiences of the body. The journal is operated through its parent organization, the Association for Public Religion and Intellectual Life (APRIL), an interreligious network of academics, activists, artists, and community leaders seeking to engage the many ways religion meets the public. Contributions to the journal exist at the nexus of religion, education, the arts, and social justice. The journal is published quarterly on behalf of the Association for Public Religion and Intellectual Life by the University of North Carolina Press.

The Association for Public Religion and Intellectual Life (formerly ARIL) is a global network of leaders, scholars, and social change agents who explore religious life, engage in intellectual inquiry, and lead ethical action in the world today. Their primary objective, especially through annual summer colloquia, the online magazine *The Commons*, and the scholarly *CrossCurrents* journal, is to bring together leading voices of our time to advocate for justice and to examine global spiritual and interreligious currents in both historical and contemporary perspectives.

Information for subscribers: Institutional print-only subscriptions are available for $250/annually. Institutional digital ($250) and digital/print ($300) subscriptions are available through Project MUSE.

A membership to APRIL includes access to *CrossCurrents* starting with Volume 58, 2008, though our partners at Project MUSE, monthly newsletters, early access to summer colloquium themes, a 40% discount on UNC Press books, and more. Membership rates are listed below:
    Regular Membership with Digital Subscription: $55
    Seminary or Student Membership with Digital Subscription: $50
    Regular Membership with Print and Digital Subscription: $95
    Seminary or Student Membership with Print and Digital Subscription: $90

We have a partnership with Duke University Press (DUP) for membership fulfillment and subscriptions. Agencies are eligible for a discount on the institutional rate. If you have questions about an existing subscription or membership please contact DUP Journals Services:
    Email subscriptions@dukeupress.edu
    Phone toll-free in the US and Canada (888) 651-0122
    Phone (919) 688-5134
    Duke University Press Journal Services, Box 90660, Durham, NC 27708

Postmaster: Send all address changes to UNC Press, c/o Duke University Journal Services, 905 W. Main St. Ste 18-B, Durham, NC 27701.

© 2024 Association for Public Religion and Intellectual Life. All rights reserved.
For more information about APRIL and *CrossCurrents*, visit https://www.aprilonline.org/

EDITOR

S. Brent Rodriguez-Plate
Hamilton College, USA

CULTURAL CONNECTIONS EDITORS

Rosalind Hinton
Independent scholar, USA
Hussein Rashid
Independent scholar, USA

ASSOCIATE EDITORS

Amanullah de Sondy
University College Cork, Ireland
Timothy K. Beal
Case Western Reserve, USA
Melanie Barbato
University of Münster, Germany

EDITORIAL BOARD

Fatimah Ashrif
Rumi's Circle; Muslim Institute, UK
Julia Watts Belser
Georgetown University, USA
Joy Bostic
Case Western Reserve, USA
Cláudio Carvalhaes
Union Seminary, USA
Judy Chen
Buddhist Council of NY and the American Buddhist Confederation, Canada
Robbie B. H. Goh
National University Singapore, Singapore
Henry Goldschmidt
Interfaith Center of New York, USA
Nikky-Guninder Singh
Colby College, USA
Scott Holland
Bethany Seminary, USA
Jonathan Homrighausen
Duke University
Erling Hope
Artist, USA
Amir Hussain
Loyola Maymount University, USA
Robert P. Jones
Public Religion Research Institute, USA
Björn Krondorfer
Northern Arizona University, USA
J. Shawn Landres
Jumpstart Labs, Santa Monica, USA
Laura Levitt
Temple University, USA
Peter Manseau
Smithsonian Institution, USA
Andrea Miller
Writer, Editor at Lion's Roar
Shabana Mir
American Islamic College, USA

Jolyon Mitchell
University of Edinburgh, UK
Diane L. Moore
Harvard University, USA
Harold Morales
Morgan State University, USA
Vanessa Ochs
University of Virginia, USA
Laurie L. Patton
Middlebury College, USA
Daria Pezzoli-Olgiati
Ludwig Maximilian University, Germany
Kathryn Reklis
Fordham University, USA
Christian Scharen
St. Lydia's Church, Brooklyn, US
Randall Styers
University of North Carolina, Chapel Hill, USA
Kayla Renée Wheeler
Xavier University, USA
Pamela Winfield
Elon University, USA
Homayra Ziad
Johns Hopkins University, USA

APRIL BOARD OF DIRECTORS

PRESIDENT
Stephanie Mitchem
VICE-PRESIDENT
Björn Krondorfer
SECRETARY
Pamela Winfield
TREASURER
Judy Chen
EXECUTIVE DIRECTOR
S. Brent Rodriguez-Plate

Julia Watts Belser
Jonah Boyarin
Shabana Mir
Randall G. Styers
Sofia Ali-Khan

PUBLISHING WITH *CROSSCURRENTS*

Articles: Each issue includes 4-8 main essays, generally on a theme, though we will also publish unsolicited submissions. If you have questions or are interested in submitting an article for review, please contact the editor, Brent Rodriguez-Plate, splate@hamilton.edu

Cultural Connections: This section includes book reviews as well as reviews of film, television, museum exhibitions, and any place we see religion meeting the public. If you have an idea for a review of any current cultural works, please contact Hussein Rashid hr@husseinrashid.com and/or Rosalind Hinton rosalindhinton@mac.com

We will occasionally publish poetry and short creative writing.

crosscurrents

VOLUME 73 : NUMBER 4 : DECEMBER 2023

**SPECIAL ISSUE: GARDENING AS SOCIAL-SPIRITUAL PRACTICE,
EDITED BY JOHAN ROELAND**

ARTICLES

361   Gardening as Social-Spiritual Practice:
An Introduction to the Special Issue
JOHAN ROELAND

364   Gardening Without a Garden
KATHRYN REKLIS

377   Queer Gardens
JOOST EMMERIK

391   Planting by Faith: A Hopi Farmer's Perspective
MICHAEL KOTUTWA JOHNSON

395   Unsettled: On Learning to Honor Powerful Strangers in an
"Immigrant World"
MEGHANN ORMOND

407   Terra-Therapy or, Growing Deep Peace
JON PAHL

420   The Slow Garden: Gardening as Deceleration
JOHAN ROELAND

POETRY

427   Children of Space
ROW LIGHT

CULTURAL CONNECTIONS

429   Ebony G. Patterson at the New York Botanical Garden:
Enter Vultures
Review by IRINA SHEYNFELD

438 Shenila Khoja-Moolji, *Rebuilding Community: Displaced Women and the Making of a Shia Ismaili Muslim Sociality*
Review by SAHIR DEWJI

443 Hadia Mubarak, *Rebellious Wives, Neglectful Husbands: Controversies in Modern Qur'anic Commentaries.*
Review by NURA SOPHIA LIEPSNER

447 Theresa A. Yugar, Sarah E. Robinson, Lilian Dube, and Teresia Mbari Hinga, eds. *Valuing Lives, Healing Earth: Religion, Gender, and Life on Earth.*
Review by TELESIA K. MUSILI

451 CONTRIBUTORS

454 ERRATA

JOHAN ROELAND

GARDENING AS SOCIAL-SPIRITUAL PRACTICE
An Introduction to the Special Issue

In our troubled world, endangered by serious challenges of climate change, conflict, inequality, and violence, the garden may not seem to be the most urgent place of scholarly attention, and gardening not the most urgent practice to pay attention to. Nevertheless, the authors in this special issue, all academics who frequently turn to the garden and find themselves connecting to the natural world through gardening, do find something very meaningful and important in these little green and vulnerable spots.

This special issue started with a conversation I had with Brent Rodríguez-Plate, the editor of this journal. We met each other in a digital meeting on film and religion and we—both scholars working in the field of religion—found that we had much in common in terms of research interests: a lived religion approach, paying attention to the material side of religion, an interest in film, and even an interest in gardening. I told Brent about my little side-project on the spirituality of gardening and my worries about this project, including what I called its "lack of complexity." I wrote that my research among gardeners kept coming back to a very simple idea (I even used the word "cliché"): people get stuck in their working lives, and in the garden, they find a way of coping with an accelerating culture. Brent then replied: "Living in the academic environments that we do, I can understand why you worry about your research, and that you fear some perceived lack of 'complexity.' To be honest, the older I get, the more I realize that so much of what is important actually does come down to some overused clichés." Months later, we finished this special issue on gardening as a social-spiritual practice, together with a great team of authors who have actually managed to both carefully unpack so-called clichés about gardening and describe the complexity and multi-layeredness of a practice that is found all over the world.

Gardening is often perceived as a hobby and a leisure activity. People love gardening, and gardening has much to offer: being outside, a connection with nature, enjoying the beauty of flowers, contributing to acts of creation, physical labor, and the satisfaction of eating the fruits of that labor. For many people, however, gardening is much more than a hobby. Small-scale farming and local gardening can be activities for alternative socio-political action, as community gardens help people take some control of their own food sources, invest practitioners with a sense of dignity, and create public spaces for communities. In many religious cultures, the garden is a sacred and mythical place, and gardening a ritualistic act of connecting to the spirits.

Many of these more-than-leisure dimensions are discussed in this special issue. In our call for proposals, we asked for essays that "mix the personal and the political, the spiritual and the social, contributing to ways we might think through gardening practices in light of religious renewal, social justice, and public futures." All authors, academics who know from experience what it is like to dig into the ground with their bare hands, have been faithful to this principle—not only thematically, but also in style: many contributions mix the personal and the academic; the rich and concrete language of personal embodied practices and the more abstract language of social and cultural theory; the individual experience of being in the garden and the analysis of gardening as a more than individual being in the world. For each author, writing about gardening and gardens is a way of relating to bigger issues: violence and peace (Jon Pahl), queerness and sexuality (Joost Emmerik), class and property (Kathryn Reklis), migration and identity (Meghann Ormond), capitalism and its "culture of speed" (Johan Roeland), and spirituality and regenerative agriculture (Michael Kotutwa Johnson).

Does gardening change anything in this world or offer an opportunity to deal with the big challenges of our age? Probably not. Or, at least not directly. Probably the old forces of domination, capitalism, and colonialism continue their devastating work on everything that is vulnerable in this world, including gardens and the practice of gardening. But quite likely something else is also happening right now: a silent revolution of people who are connected, like trees, invisible and underground. People who are able to communicate, because they are wired like roots of trees and they feel, like trees, the needs and vulnerabilities of others. People who are grounded and as such in tune with the earth because they know they are earth. People who know that human grounding and "earthing" is complex and layered and that neglecting injustice and inequality does not create a healthy soil for the common flourishing of people and planet.

The garden is much more than a place of leisure, and gardening is much more than an innocent, apolitical, or anti-social hobby. While gardens are often pleasurable places and gardening can certainly be a pleasant practice, serious issues are at stake in the garden: issues regarding the way we relate to ourselves and our own humanity; to others and our shared humanity; to the planet and our shared vulnerability; to what is sacred in this world.

KATHRYN REKLIS

GARDENING WITHOUT A GARDEN

"[T]he garden for me is so bound up with words about the garden, with words themselves, that any set idea of the garden, any set picture, is a provocation to me."
—Jamaica Kincaid[1]

"In this time of diminished expectation, I look for disturbance-based ecologies in which many species sometimes live together without either harmony or conquest."
—Anna Lowenhaupt Tsing[2]

I gotta get out of bed and get a hammer and a nail
Learn how to use my hands, not just my head
I think myself into jail
Now I know a refuge never grows
From a chin in a hand in a thoughtful pose
Gotta tend the earth if you want a rose
— Indigo Girls[3]

In the early days of the Covid pandemic, my family and I drove from our small Queens apartment to a historic house museum in Brooklyn to pick up milk crate planters full of soil. JetBlue Airline had hundreds of them that could no longer be tended at their JFK terminal, and a community group was giving them away in the hope that they would not go to waste. I signed up to collect crates with a sense of urgency. This was the moment I had long been waiting for: the chance to try my hand at gardening—or at least a form of growing something in soil—which I felt implicitly was a good lacking from my life, and maybe even a necessity given the state of the world.

It is hard to put into words how close a sense of apocalypse sat next to the skin of everyday life in late April 2020 in New York City, a thin membrane (of hope? of denial?) keeping at bay thoughts of civilizational collapse. For weeks we would open our windows to break the stifling air only to shut them again when the constant wail of ambulances overwhelmed our five-year-old daughter. We began plotting our daily family walks to avoid the morgue trucks parked on streets just blocks from our apartment. My children didn't leave our home for a full day of school, camp, or time with friends for 486 days.

It wasn't so much that I thought I'd be able to grow food to feed my family in a few milk crates perched precariously on the porch of our small second-floor apartment. I thought of the pandemic as a dress rehearsal, a chance to be better prepared next time. Gardening is a useful skill, I would think, one that would make me a valuable and contributing community member in the coming social upheavals and ecological catastrophes. The inverse of this longing was the terrified suspicion that I would have nothing of value to offer my fellow survivors if I couldn't even grow food—if I didn't even know how to prepare the soil for potential growth.[4] A garden would also be a source of soul-making, a kind of slow labor that would rewire my body and brain to different temporal rhythms than the death-dealing grind of late capitalism; it would teach me a different way to be a member of my species among other species.[5] A garden would help me avert the apocalypse or it would help me prepare for it—not just practically in terms of hard skills I might need for survival or as part of a process of weaning myself off the agricultural industrial complex, but in terms of the kind of animal I would learn to be in a shifting, fragile ecosystem. The pandemic was a siren in the night, both the storm and the reprieve from it, a chance to catch one's breath, root one's feet, train one's hands: who knew what else was coming?

The milk crates were a failure. Despite the blazing sun of that summer, the porch didn't get enough light for anything to grow. Every night of that first fall and winter, as my partner and I attempted to teach five college classes, first grade, and fifth grade out of our 800-square-foot apartment, I would come to the porch and weep in the darkness while the mental health of my children plunged off a cliff, wondering how we would all wake up and do it again the next day. If my life was a fairy tale, my tears might have watered the fledgling carrot seeds, my sorrow given root to the struggling parsley. I might have woken up to abundance soaked in the miraculous, perhaps imbued with the properties we needed to survive, or to escape. I finally gave the crates to a friend with a small backyard and plenty of light. Carrots, parsley, cucumbers, and even some small peppers grew rapidly in those better conditions. And that was my first lesson in gardening without a garden.

*****

The friend who gave me the seeds to plant in my milk crates is a self-professed Appalachian granny, which in some times and places would make her a witch. She was very patient in explaining that I couldn't just plant all my seeds at once, nor should I, she cautioned, attempt to plant anything right away. We were in a fourth quarter moon, a good time to prepare soil but a very unproductive time for planting. Carrots like to be planted in a third quarter moon, so I would need to wait nearly a month for those. But parsley is best planted in a first quarter moon.[6] I will admit that I didn't follow her advice. I wasn't sure if I believed her. We both saw the results of my foolishness: I failed, whereas she continues to grow vegetables on her apartment fire escape and keeps a healthy herb garden growing in pots in her kitchen for medicinal and spiritual purposes.

In the second spring of the pandemic, she invited several women who had formed a survival collective to go on plant-gathering walks with her around our neighborhood. Our main task was looking for mugwort. Mugwort (*Artemisia vulgaris*), she taught me, is a plant native to Europe and East Asia that now grows abundantly in North America, having been introduced by settler colonists. Mugwort is referenced in Anglo-Saxon, Old Norse, and German sources dating back over a thousand years. In addition to being used medicinally to treat burns, insect bites, itching, bruises, fevers, coughs, menstrual pain, and respiratory ailments, it is believed to have spiritual and magical properties.[7] It was widely believed by medieval Europeans that John the Baptist wore a mugwort girdle in the wilderness, and the association with St. John reinforced the belief that the plant gave protection against evil spirits and misfortune.[8]

My friend uses mugwort in many of her medicines and kitchen spells both because it has a long history of use in Appalachian herbal medicine, and, she explained, because she identifies with its invasive tendencies. As a white descendent of settler colonists, she feels a special kinship with invasive plants. So much white magic, she explained, attempts to appropriate Indigenous or non-European traditions. She won't use sage, especially white sage, for this reason, or other plants that are strongly identified with lineages that are not her own. "White people think they have to appropriate everything," she told me once, because white people have been taught that they don't have any culture but whiteness, which is an invented ideology of pillage and supremacy and death. "It's not like we can just reject whiteness and be done with it," she said, "but white people must heal from whiteness too." Recognizing herself in kinship with the invasive plants in her ecosystem forces her to work against the harms of invasion. Once mugwort grew plentifully in North America, many Indigenous American groups made use of it for medicinal and spiritual purposes, much like pre-Christian Europeans adapted their own usage to a new Christian mythology. Spiritual currents are rarely smooth or linear, but ecological and spiritual balance comes from working with those currents instead of ignoring them.

Ecological balance is hard to come by in our neighborhood, which is home to the Ravenswood Generating Station, colloquially known as Big Allis. When it was built in 1965 it was the world's first million kilowatt power plant and had the capacity to supply 21% of the power for New York City.[9] The plant is surrounded by three major public housing projects, including Queensbridge Houses, the largest public housing project in North America, and Ravenswood Houses, my neighbors across the street.[11] Not incidentally, our neighborhood is also known as "asthma alley," with childhood asthma rates much higher than any other neighborhood in Queens.[11] We also have one of the lowest number of sidewalk trees when compared to most other neighborhoods surrounding us.[12]

I never thought much about the frequency of sidewalk trees until I moved to Queens with my one-year-old. He was born on the Upper West Side, in a neighborhood with approximately 6,000 more trees than our neighborhood in Queens, far lower rates of childhood asthma, and abundant playgrounds with well-maintained sandboxes, fountains, and swings. There were no sandboxes in our new playgrounds, but anytime he was out of a stroller he would squat down in the hardpacked dirt near a sidewalk tree and start poking, digging, and patting. I would scan quickly for broken glass and cigarette butts, often removing some of both, and then stand awkwardly as other people looked askance as they walked by. Like most upper-middle-class white mothers of my generation, I had a general sense that I was supposed to let him follow his natural curiosity, especially if it was connected to nature, and I tried to ignore the cognitive dissonance of following this mantra as my kid poked his hands through layers of dog piss and stale beer.

Even then, when confronted with the dirt of these trees, it was not until these mugwort walks that I recognized these spaces as land. A tree planted in the sidewalk is a reminder that the bare facets of the city are held together by the sheer force of human invasion into other ecosystems. The miles of concrete and asphalt that are the natural habitat of human life on an urban scale are layered on top of earth, which peeks through as "nature" in these strange patches of dirt that support a tree. In my mind, the square of urban dirt turned to raw earth and hidden land when I realized the dirt grew things. This sounds so simple when I write it here, but this change in perception was revelatory at the time. I never thought about how trees could grow out of concrete in the first place.

Many sidewalk trees don't take root, and this is often why the city neglects planting them in lower-income neighborhoods. Unless people demand them and their demands are recognized as legitimate, it is an expensive prospect to plant a tree that might not survive. The more I started paying attention, the more miraculous trees growing out of the sidewalk began to seem. I started to notice all the other growth that developed around them—weeds and small shrubs, occasional flowers, and even some mugwort—seeds deposited by birds or blown by wind, finding unexpected earth. These are refugee plants, often surrounded by human refuse. Around most sidewalk trees in my neighborhood, you can find trash of all kinds—fast food wrappers, cigarette butts, old liquor bottles, unidentifiable scraps of paper that might have been blown as far as the seeds of the weeds they are now nestled among.

In her study of the global circulation of the matsutake mushroom trade, Anna Tsing urges us to notice the way global capitalism has concentrated wealth by "making both humans and nonhumans into resources for investment" by alienating living things from their living environments, but also the way "many species sometimes live together without either harmony or conquest," without the assumption of progress or accumulation.[13] I began to think of the patches of earth at the base of a sidewalk tree as tiny microcosms of interspecies living without harmony or conquest. The invasive human species has created conditions that are hostile not only to many other ecological systems but also to many forms of human life. Nothing should grow in asphalt. Human children shouldn't grow up next to power plants that poison their oxygen. There are not enough sidewalk trees in all of New York City to restore the carbon cycle of the planetary system. Still, we breathe better with the trees than without them, and even trees surrounded by the refuse of many different ecologies force an encounter with the land.

*****

On a small street that leads from a major commercial avenue to my apartment there are two sidewalk trees that are particularly luscious examples of the symbiosis of refuse. The trees are extravagant in their springtime foliage, branches sagging under an abundance of dark, thick leaves and fragrant buds. I must duck my head to walk under the branches. For a split second, I can look up and be completely enveloped in green. The small patches of land where they have taken root are always littered with trash and a serious collection of weed grasses, both growing thicker each week as summer comes and no one cares for this land.

The sidewalk is relatively narrow on this street, and within two or three feet of the tree is a chain link fence that marks off a few one- and two-family homes. These homes do not have yards to speak of, though there are tiny patches of land left when the concrete was poured to make room for several small driveways. Multiple rose bushes grow out of each patch, spilling over the fence and brushing my arms if I step out of the way of the trees.

This wild, riotous beauty is the most visible form of gardening in my neighborhood. Much of western Queens is, as a friend once put it to me, "architecturally spotty." We don't have wide avenues lined with brownstones or stately apartment buildings. While certain streets reflect the hallmarks of organized design—a block of uniform one- or symmetrical two-family homes, for example—the next street will be a hodge-podge of pre-war apartment buildings, vinyl-sided single-family row houses, and brick multi-families jammed next to each other with only small slivers of space for a driveway or a side alley. Those with access to small front or side yards often plant flower gardens or even small fruit trees. But most human cultivation takes place in planters on porches, stoops, and balconies.

Perhaps to make up for this visual discontinuity, my neighbors tend toward a maximalist floral aesthetic. It is not uncommon to see a porch almost completely covered with colorful plastic planters overflowing with bright flowers of all kinds. Many people build wooden trellises over small walkways and cover them with flowering vines or hang potted flowers from their poles or along the edges of balconies.

Gardens are often divided into one of two types: ornamental—ranging across historical periods and geographies in style and form[14]—and practical, such as the "kitchen garden," which refers to designated plots of land close to private residences maintained for the express purpose of growing food necessary for cooking or plants needed for medical remedies.[15] Both varieties persist in contemporary American gardening practice: in flower gardens maintained largely for aesthetic purposes and vegetable gardens grown in backyards and side plots for supplementary, or superlative food.

That phrase, "superlative food," points to the fact that, as one scholar puts it, while "in some areas with poor access to retail food, gardens may be relied upon as a food source, . . . anyone who has gardened will testify that it is not cheaper to grow food oneself, at least not in developed countries."[16] Nonetheless, Gordon Campbell argues, even if you can concretely prove to gardeners that it is more costly to grow their own food than to buy it, they would not cease in their gardening practices and would almost certainly maintain their preference for the not-strictly-necessary food that they grow themselves.[17] So, perhaps, then, we might say that in parts of the world where most food is or could be acquired without personal access to land all gardens are ornamental, whether they are displaying carrots or roses.

In Tsitsi Dangarembga's novel *Nervous Conditions*, the narrator, Tambu, describes her first encounter with an ornamental garden: "I too could think of planting things for merrier reasons than the chore of keeping breath in the body. . . . Our home would answer well to being cheered up by such lovely flowers. Bright and cheery, they had been planted for joy. What a strange idea that was. It was a liberation."[18] Until this point in the novel, gardening was not satisfying work. It brings the narrator neither joy nor self-determination nor self-sufficiency. It is brutal labor that leads to nothing but suffering. I first encountered Dangarembga's work in Jamaica Kincaid's writing about gardening, which is both a collection of autobiographical reflections on her own gardening practice and a startling retelling of colonial history through a botanical and geographical lens. "What is the relationship between gardening and conquest?" Kincaid asks in the chapter where she discusses Tambu's story. "At what moment does such ordinary, everyday beauty become a luxury?" And under what conditions does "growing just for the sheer joy of it" become liberation?[19]

Halfway through the first three years of the Covid pandemic, my family and I moved from a two-bedroom, second-floor apartment inside a three-family home into a three-bedroom apartment in a co-op building a few blocks away. The co-op was built in 1950 as a middle-income housing complex across the street from the Ravenswood Houses, twin prongs of an urban planning experiment to provide affordable housing along a hierarchical scale of deserving need. Wealthy Manhattanites sat on the original board of our co-op and were actively involved in supporting public housing projects for the less fortunate down the wealth ladder. Co-operative housing for the middle class and public housing for the deserving poor were both "slum-clearing" initiatives.[20] Their benevolence did not extend to zoning protections that would block environmental pollution like Big Allis, of course, but the waste of capitalism's excess must go somewhere, and the hierarchy of deserving need is inverted when it comes to who deserves protection, health, and peace.[21]

Surrounding these two massive housing projects are several blocks of smaller apartment buildings and single- and multi-family homes. By the second half of the twentieth century, most of these homes had shifted hands from Italian and Greek immigrant families who moved out to Long Island to pursue the American dream of suburban houses with real yards. Today, most of these houses are owned by South Asian and Middle Eastern families. I learned some of this history from the couple who ran the family daycare both our children attended out of their family home. He was Iranian, she was Pakistani: a true Queens love match. Her mother bought the house in the 1960s and it had provided a clear path into the middle class for her, her new husband, and their daughter, who we knew from the time she was a middle schooler up until she went to college. Because of the daycare, their gardening was a bit more subdued than that of other neighbors, but they had a trellis covered in roses and lilacs that ran wild through the small backyard where the children played on warm days.

I do not know what histories of immigration and translation might have inspired my neighbors from Bengal, Bangladesh, India, Pakistan, Iran, and Iraq to take on a maximalist floral aesthetic in their gardening. Was it a trend that someone started and others followed? Did it carry a significance obscured to me, a relative newcomer to the neighborhood? Nor can I tell you if they, like Tambu, receive sheer joy from the wild bounty of their potted gardens. But I can speak of the joy their extravagance provides for me, as someone who does not have a garden or a porch, or even a stoop, and whose tastes have been warped by decades of exposure to hipster minimalism. Even the most mundane of daily walks takes me through these gardens that refuse to obey laws of tidy enclosure, enveloping me in beauty that feels like luxury, a gift of sharing space.

*****

The English word "garden" and its companion "yard" come from the Old English for "fence" or "enclosure,"[22] and gardens are therefore intimately tied to histories of land usage and shifting debates about private versus public land and access to natural resources. When we think of contemporary gardening in America, most of us probably imagine a one-family home with access to a front or back yard. Gardens, in this imagining, are hobbies for a shrinking class of suburban homeowners, and almost certainly part of a cultural matrix that is contributing to the uninhabitability of the earth.[23] But there is a much older history of gardening related to the idea of the commons that has never completely fallen out of practice.

"The commons" is a shorthand often used to refer to patterns of land and resource usage prior to the advent of private property as we know it today. In England, for example, while land might technically have belonged to lords, the crown, or the church, its use for growing food was allotted to commoners according to their need. A large open field or pasture abutted by forests might have allotments for growing until the harvest season was over, when the land would remain available for common access—to permit the collection of firewood, fishing in streams, grazing of livestock, or rooting of pigs.[24] The first English settlers in the North American colonies brought these assumptions about the commons with them, even as many colonists profited from new enclosure laws that criminalized vagrancy and common land use.[25] Those settlers discovered that the Wampanoag, among whom they settled, shared a non-possessive idea of land use. As Eula Biss has noted, "rights to use the same plot of land could overlap, so that one family might hold the right to fish in a stream and another might hold the right to farm the banks of that stream. Usage rights could be passed down from mothers to daughters, but the land itself could not be possessed."[26]

We might think of the form of subsistence agriculture practiced in the commons as gardens without enclosure, so perhaps these are not gardens at all in the etymological sense. The "kitchen garden," or potager, is the antecedent to what we might think of as the vegetable garden, and it implied a private plot of land connected to a private residence for the purpose of growing food for the household. Peasants didn't have "gardens" in this sense because they didn't have private property. The advent of private property through acts of enclosure both destroyed the commons—as a legally recognized system of allocating rights for land and resource use—and, perhaps, gave birth to the garden as we know it.

When I think of it now, I realize that what I wanted from gardening in those early days of the pandemic was really the commons—a way of thinking about access to the resources necessary for both survival and meaningful life. It is another way of thinking about how we interact with the resources of land and common space, how we inhabit space shared with each other and other species. In the age of private property and broken supply chains we are caught in this in-between: no one can just call the commons into being through sheer desire, but living without them is unsustainable. And so, for me, gardening without a garden is a way of naming a longing for a spatial or material commons, a kind of gardening that does not require everyone to have their own plot of land or private enclosed space.

In giving my milk crates to a neighbor with access to better sunlight and then sharing the bounty of that harvest, we were striving toward a kind of commons. In the early months of the pandemic, when the city became a wide-open space again, that same neighbor used to walk the abandoned beaches of the Far Rockaways and would occasionally find huge beds of mussels washed up on shore, a bounty made newly available as overharvesting receded under pandemic restrictions. She would deliver beds of mussels to neighbors, which we would exchange for hand-mixed cocktails or freshly baked goods. We rigged up a basket and pulley system from our second-floor porch to facilitate socially distanced exchanges. The network of exchanges multiplied, with neighbors—some we knew well and some we had never met—bringing food grown or scavenged or made to share with each other, left on porches and stoops.

Out of these exchanges grew much deeper networks of solidarity and exchange that introduced me to some actual gardens and gardening collectives. A group of my neighbors have worked for years to restore a colonial era cemetery and repurpose much of its adjacent land as a community garden.[27] Another group, without a web presence, has planted a meditation and herbal/medicinal garden in the Astoria Houses, the third public housing project that surrounds Big Allis. Our new co-op is full of long-time Queens gardeners, mostly older white women who maintain small garden beds around our common space and who invite volunteers to help them tend the plants. With all these neighbors, my children and I have cleared land, dug garden beds, prepared soil boxes, arranged rock formations, and learned how to weed.

In these ways, I have acquired many gardens, and I am, slowly, learning the skills I imagined I would need to face whatever future is coming. Still, I wouldn't count on myself to grow the food needed to survive a future apocalypse, nor have I learned new animal rhythms by following the life cycle of a plant. What I needed and wanted in my longings for a garden are things I have learned without a garden: how to see the land, and beauty, and ecological entanglement; what it means to share life and depend on other forms of life; how to make private space public and move through public space as if it were shared.

I read and think more about gardens than is reasonable for someone who will probably never have a garden of my own. Gardens are for me, as Kincaid says in the first epigraph of this essay, "bound up with words about the garden, with words themselves." Like words, like language, gardens occupy a strange space between activity and passivity. Gardens, like language, name the human activity of conscious cultivation, for necessity and, if we are lucky, also for joy. Cultivation implies action: hands in the earth, words in a song, pen to the page. But growing anything means passivity too, encountering life systems and timescales beyond effortful control, inheritance in earth and syntax. Gardens and language are about the commons, about what Earth's species have in common with one another and how we choose to entangle our lives in common survival and flourishing. Maybe also like language, which is a necessity of life and thought in common, we can't help but be gardeners whether we have a garden or not.

NOTES
1. Kincaid, *My Garden (Book)*, 7.
2. Tsing, *The Mushroom at the End of the World*, 5.
3. Indigo Girls, "Hammer and Nail."
4. The urgency of this desire was nurtured with practical suggestions for skill development by the third season of the podcast *How to Survive the End of the World*.
5. Odell, *Saving Time*, 81–115.
6. She was following Wigginton, ed., *Foxfire* 2, 212–27.
7. Wigginton, ed., *Foxfire* 2, 274–303.
8. Grieve, *A Modern Herbal*, 858.
9. Roosevelt Island Historical Society, "Let's Explain What is Happening in Ravenswood."
10. The non-coincidental nature of this placement could be interpreted in conversation with Bullard, *Confronting Environmental Racism*. See esp. 15–24; 38–39.

11. "The New York City Community Air Survey"; Misdary, "Goodbye Big Allis?".
12. NYC Tree Map.
13. Tsing, *The Mushroom at the End of the World*, 5.
14. Thacker, *The History of Gardens*; Carroll, Earthly Paradises.
15. Wilson, *The Country House Kitchen Garden*, 27–45.
16. Norwood, "The Garden as Art, Hobby, and the Good Life," 304–12.
17. Campbell, *Garden History*, 1–4.
18. Dangarembga, *Nervous Conditions*, 187.
19. Kincaid, *My Garden (Book)*, 116–17.
20. Pink, "Queensview."
21. Pellow, *Resisting Global Toxics*, 9.
22. Turner, *Garden History*, 1–3.
23. Learn, "Your Perfect Lawn is Bad for the Environment"; Ramirez, "Why the Great American Lawn is Terrible for the West's Water Crisis."
24. Linebaugh and Rediker, *The Many-Headed Hydra*, 22–24.
25. Linebaugh and Rediker, *The Many-Headed Hydra*, 24–26.
26. Biss, "The Theft of the Commons."
27. The Moore Jackson Community Garden and Cemetery: https://www.moorejacksonnyc.org/

REFERENCES

Biss, Eula. "The Theft of the Commons." *New Yorker*, June 8, 2022. https://www.newyorker.com/culture/essay/the-theft-of-the-commons.

Brown, Autumn, and adrienne maree brown. *How to Survive the End of the World*. Season 3. Podcast audio. April 17–June 12, 2020. https://www.endoftheworldshow.org.

Bullard, Robert. *Confronting Environmental Racism: Voices from the Grassroots*. Boston: South End Press, 1993.

Campbell, Gordon. *Garden History: A Very Short Introduction*. New York: Oxford University Press, 2019.

Carroll, Maureen. *Earthly Paradises: Ancient Gardens in History and Archaeology*. London: British Museum Press, 1986.

Dangarembga, Tsitsi. *Nervous Conditions.* New York: Faber, 2021.

Grieve, Maud. *A Modern Herbal: The Medicinal, Culinary, Cosmetic and Economic Properties, Cultivation and Folklore of Herbs, Grasses, Fungi, Shrubs, & Trees with All Their Modern Scientific Uses*. Vol. 2. London: Dover Publications, 1971.

Hersey, Tricia. *Rest is Resistance: A Manifesto*. New York: Little, Brown, 2022.

Indigo Girls. "Hammer and Nail." Released 1990. Track 1 on *Nomads, Indians, Saints*. Epic, vinyl.

Learn, Joshua Lapp. "Your Perfect Lawn Is Bad for the Environment. Here's What to Do Instead." *Discover Magazine*, May 29, 2021. https://www.discovermagazine.com/environment/your-perfect-lawn-is-bad-for-the-environment-heres-what-to-do-instead.

Linebaugh, Peter and Marcus Rediker. *The Many-Headed Hydra: Sailors, Slaves, Commoners, and the Hidden History of the Revolutionary Atlantic*. Boston: Beacon, 2013.

Kincaid, Jamaica. *My Garden (Book)*. New York: Farrar Straus & Giroux, 1999.

Misdary, Rosemary. "Goodbye Big Allis? NYC's Largest Power Plant Sets Course for 100% Renewable Energy." *The Gothamist*, September 1, 2022. https://gothamist.com/news/goodbye-big-allis-nycs-largest-power-plant-sets-course-for-100-renewable-energy.

"The New York City Community Air Survey: Neighborhood Air Quality 2008–2019." New York City Department of Health and Mental Hygiene, 2021. https://nyccas.cityofnewyork.us/nyccas2021v9/report/2.

New York City Department of Parks & Recreation. "NYC Tree Map." Accessed June 5, 2023. https://tree-map.nycgovparks.org.

Norwood, F. Bailey. "The Garden as Art, Hobby, and the Good Life." *HortTechnology* 32, no. 3 (2022): 304–12. https://doi.org/10.21273/HORTTECH05026-22.

Odell, Jenny. *Saving Time: Discovering a Life Beyond the Clock*. New York: Random House, 2023.

Pellow, David N. *Resisting Global Toxics: Transnational Movements for Environmental Justice*. Cambridge, MA: MIT Press, 2007.

Pink, Louis H. "Queensview: How this Pioneering Co-Operative Housing Project in Long Island City is Functioning – it's history and importance to cities working on slum-clearance programs," *The American City*, 1952. https://queensvw.com/archives-1952-queensview-article-by-louis-pink.

Ramirez, Rachel. Why the Great American Lawn is Terrible for the West's Water Crisis." CNN, April 29, 2022. https://www.cnn.com/2022/04/28/us/why-grass-lawns-are-bad-for-drought-water-crisis-climate/index.html.

Roosevelt Island Historical Society. "Let's Explain What is Happening in Ravenswood." November 20, 2020. https://rihs.us/2020/11/12/thursday-november-12-2020-lets-explain-what-is-happening-in-ravenswood.

Thacker, Christopher, *The History of Gardens*. Berkeley: University of California Press, 1979.

Tsing, Anna Lowenhaupt. *The Mushroom at the End of the World: On the Possibility of Life in Capitalist Ruins*. Princeton, NJ: Princeton University Press, 2021.

Turner, Tom. Garden History: *Philosophy and Design 2000 BC–2000 AD*. New York: Routledge, 2004.

Wigginton, Eliot, editor. Foxfire 2: *Ghost Stories, Spring Wild Plant Foods, Spinning and Weaving, Midwifing, Burial Customs, Corn Shuckin's, Wagon Making and More Affairs of Plain Living*. Albany, NY: Anchor Press, 1973.

Wilson, C. Anne. *The Country House Kitchen Garden 1600–1950: How Produce Was Grown and How It Was Used*. London: Sutton, 1998.

JOOST EMMERIK

QUEER GARDENS

MY GRANDMOTHER'S ALLOTMENT
During my childhood, we called my grandmother Kleine Oma, "little grandma," because she was shorter and thinner than my other grandmother. Kleine Oma tended to an allotment garden on the outskirts of The Hague. As a child, it was the only garden in my life that I visited several times a year. I grew up in an upstairs city apartment. For me, gardens were always the domain of others, something to be looked at from above. We had a balcony, with some plants, where we sat in the sun and read books. But that was about it.

Within the confines of her allotment garden, Kleine Oma had created a world of her own, a personal microcosm with grass, gravel tiles, perennials, some fruit trees, and a little cabin. I vividly remember the large garden chest, with a lid so heavy I wasn't able to lift it alone. The lid was covered in tar, and when the summer sun shone on it, the smell of tar filled the garden. Today, the smell of a street being asphalted still takes me back to the garden of my grandmother.

For me the garden was magical—a place unlike any other in my everyday lifeworld, different from the upstairs apartment where I grew up, my school, or the street where I lived. In the garden I could mess around with dirt, plants, water, and fire, things that could only be done there. These things were specifically connected to that place, the weather, and the seasons; I would use tools that only had a function in that context and words that only applied to events happening there.

I liked being outdoors, smelling, hearing, touching, seeing, and tasting things other than those in my regular lifeworld. My grandmother gave me little chores: mowing the lawn, watering plants, raking the soil. I enjoyed these actions—to me they felt like rituals, like incantations I performed in order to make the garden do what I wanted it to do. It gave me ideas for how to relate to the world outside of me. I felt safe here within the enclosed privacy of the garden, my grandmother rumbling about, cinnamon biscuits waiting on the counter.

Figure 1. My grandfather and grandmother in their allotment garden, ca. 1970. Author's family archive.

THE INDIFFERENCE OF NATURE

From an early age, I knew I was different from most other kids. And from that early age, I thought it best to behave in a "normal," normative way, in order to avoid trouble, questions, attention. I was an introverted kid; I preferred reading and drawing in my bedroom to playing outside with other kids. I did have a desire to participate in the big wide world; I just didn't know how, and I was afraid people wouldn't accept me. So I pretended to be someone I thought others expected me to be. I learned how to read a room and copy its supposed appropriate behavior, just to create a sense of safety for myself, while in the process hiding the real me.

In the garden of my grandmother, I felt safe enough to let go. Here, I didn't have to pretend to be anything other than who I was. The apple tree didn't mind me playing with dolls; the blackberry bush couldn't care less who I felt attracted to. Outside the scope of other people, in the company of trees, plants, insects, grass, and my loving grandmother, I felt safe and accepted by the world around me. I could let go of the filter of expectations my thoughts kept putting between me and the environment. This opened up another realm: a less rational, more sensorial world filled with fantasy and associations with other values. As Gilles Clément puts it:

> Outside the garden, human society is required to postpone its dreams in order to defend social status, or simply to exist. Inside the garden, existential harassment disappears: the question is no longer where to go, or which respectable conventions of behavior or appearance to obey. It is no longer a matter of adjusting to so-called modernity; the birds will not be impressed by our feats of managerial competitiveness. Being in the garden is a matter of being, and it demands silence.[1]

Author Jeremy Naydler also mentions this different set of values that are adhered to in the garden: "Life goes on in our gardens quite independently of us."[2] Or in the words of Dutch urbanist and gardener Pieter Verhagen, "[Humans] cannot live without nature in their life, even if they destroy her appearance. Conversely, nature is completely indifferent to humans, tolerates them at most as a spectator, and actually knows nothing about their existence."[3]

My grandmother's garden, and gardeners like Naydler and Verhagen, made me realize it's not the natural world that's judging me, but instead it is only humans, acting from culture, a human societal construct. For me, this opened up an enormous sense of acceptance and an enormous sense of freedom: in the garden, no one is paying much attention to me. I could be who I wanted to be. I belong, and it is a matter of simply being.

QUEER SPACES

I'm not the first queer person to experience a feeling of safety and acceptance within the confined space of the garden. Throughout history, queer people have created outdoor places, free from the norms and conventions of mainstream society—gardens as places of refuge, havens to feel safe and to express one's authentic self.

English poet and openly gay man Edward Carpenter (1844–1929) created Millthorpe, dreaming of building "a rendezvous for all classes and conditions of society."[4] Christopher Lloyd (1921–2006) created Great Dixter, a garden full of experiment and room for natural processes to happen. Then there is Jardin Majorelle, the garden of Yves St. Laurent and his partner Pierre Bergé in Marrakech; the private garden of fashion designer Dries van Noten; and the garden of Derek Jarman (1947–1994) on the Ness, closely interwoven with the surrounding landscape. Jarman's was a performative space where he was canonized in 1991 by the gay male nuns of the Sisters of Perpetual Indulgence. Closer to home, Henk Gerritsen (1948–2008) and his partner Anton Schlepers (1945–1993) created the Priona Gardens in Schuinesloot, a place full of experimentation where planting, art, and alternative ways of maintenance went hand in hand.

So, what's particularly queer about these gardens? What are queer spaces anyway? And can a garden be a queer space?

In *Queer Architecture*, Aaron Betsky talks about how "queer spaces" reflect the experiences of homosexuals in a straight culture: "Often forced to hide their true nature, gay men and women have turned inward, playing with the norms of interior space and creating environments of stagecraft and celebration where they can define themselves without fear."[5]

Evan Pavka discusses the ways queer spaces exist in contrast with normative spaces, describing the latter as "spaces where rules are very strict, but you can feel that there are other places with many different layers to them, where many things could happen. Queer, in this sense, is the possibility of behaving differently."[6] Queer, then, can be understood as "the cohesion of everything in conflict with the heterosexual capitalist world. Queer is a total rejection of the regime of the Normal."[7] And to link this to space, Pavka writes that "thinking beyond the closet and the washroom, nightclubs, bars and dance floors have also been key environments through which queer folks found safety, community and belonging."[8]

In light of these descriptions, a garden is not that different from a nightclub: you have to know where it is and how to get there. Once you've found it, you're never quite sure if you can enter or not. There's a certain door policy—a person has to grant you access. Once inside, you can experience a feeling of safety and find your peers in an environment dedicated to stagecraft and celebration. Within the safe space of the club or the garden, you've got to adhere to a specific set of rules. And within this safe space, surrounded by your community, you can experience a sense of acceptance and belonging. The above-mentioned gardens of Carpenter and Jarman all line up with these ideas of stagecraft and celebration, of places with the possibility of behaving differently, places that give a feeling of safety, community, and belonging.

Architectural historian Joe Crowdy writes how both the gardens of Carpenter and Jarman were "isolated havens, whether from Victorian morality and industrialization or Thatcherite politics and AIDS hysteria. They were both centers of pilgrimage: for devotees of their creators' writing and art, and for those drawn to alternative ways of living with plants and people." He continues to note how Jarman's garden "is not a garden snipped and strained into regimented order: plants are allowed to take up space as they please, to coalesce or grow into new forms," and mentions how "Common to both these gardens was a sympathy for 'queer' plants: weeds and overgrown shrubs of uncouth vigour." Crowdy concludes, "If the garden at Millthorpe was a manifesto, a utopian germ of new life, the garden at Prospect Cottage was a salve, a meditation on the possibility of life and beauty amid loss and decay."[9]

These gardens can be read as "environments of stagecraft and celebration," sites where guardians have created safe havens to experiment with plants, art, gender, and sexuality. They are manifestos as well as salves, and they create a place where it's safe to express one's authentic self, where queer people have found safety, community, and belonging.[10]

EXPERIMENTS, TESTS, AND ESSAYS

There are fewer things I like better than driving through the English, Italian, or German countryside, on the lookout for a garden to visit. It feels like a parallel world of care, gentility, beauty, and Victoria Sponge cake, where I never feel I have to hide my true self. I engage in conversation with random strangers about the beauty of a plant, the clever way the bin is hidden, or just about the weather. Poet Laureate Alfred Austin describes how this "collectivist perspective"[11] cuts through societal divides: "be his or her rank what it may be, in I go, opening the gate, whether a huge iron or a humble wicket, with a proud confidence, certain to find a man and a brother, a woman and a sister. I have made many a life-long friend by a bold intrusion, and instant conference over a Paeony or a Michaelmas Daisy I had not seen before."[12] It is a shared love of the natural world and wanting to partake in it that connects us, and what is so delightful to talk about. Gardens create a sense of connection,

Figure 2. The Parco dei Mostri in Bomarzo, Italy, 2020. Photo by author.

a feeling of being part of a team, a tribe, or a secret society. Differences and judgements seem to fade between all that foliage.

Some gardens I visited really stuck with me. The Parco dei Mostri in Bomarzo often lingers in my mind, as do De Geometriske Haver by Carl Theodore Sørensen in Herning and the private garden of Gudmund Nyeland Brandt in Ordrup. The private garden of Sven Ingvar Andersson in Sweden pops up often; so does the garden underneath a Paris rail track by Gilles Clement, even though I've only seen it in pictures. Martha Schwartz's Splice Garden, Greg Shepherd's Bosco della Ragnaia, Cornelia Hahn Oberlander's garden for the National Gallery of Canada,

Figure 3. The Geometric Gardens by Carl Theodor Sørensen in Herning, Denmark, 2022. Photo by author.

the mountain garden of Bér Slangen, the Dessau-Wörlitzer Gartenreich by Leopold III Friedrich Franz of Anhalt-Dessau... the list goes on and on.

But why these? What is it about these gardens that fascinates me, that somehow resonates with me? Looking back, I think it is because they are all so very different from the (hetero)normative, mainstream family garden with a trampoline, a barbecue grill, and an inflatable pool. They are not about practicalities, about keeping the kids entertained, about showing off, or keeping the neighbors satisfied.

These gardens I just mentioned function for me as queer gardens. Queer gardens are experiments, tests, essays. They're about finding a way

Figure 4. Marnas, the private garden of Sven-Ingvar Andersson in Sweden, 2022. Photo by author.

to relate to the world, a place on earth that means something to their creators, and their visitors, safe spaces in which to behave differently. They are about self-actualization and don't worry much about practicalities or, better, these practicalities are taken for granted and solved. Yet, they are so much more: they tell stories; they are beings of their own, composed of a multitude of other living beings. They're quirky, willful, playful, expressions of the characters of their creators and gardeners. They stretch the idea of what a garden can or should be and in doing so, they inspire other designers. For example, Piet Oudolf discusses the Priona Gardens of Henk Gerritsen: "Because of Henk my ideas about how to create gardens have changed drastically."[13] Gerritsen had a different opinion about what kinds of plants belonged in the garden, what was considered beautiful or appropriate at that time. He experimented with plants that were considered weeds, with letting plants grow the way they wanted instead of guiding and trimming them, with not watering plants, letting them fend for themselves. Not all visitors to his garden appreciate this ("You should water your plants! They are dying!"), but today, some forty years later, his ideas are becoming more mainstream.

MULTIPLE MEANINGS

You see a similar thing happening in garden literature; the majority of garden books are about what to plant where, how to prune, when to trim, how to compost, and what the newest cultivars are. I consider these the normative books, the books that deal with the standard things of gardening, slowly evolving within a strict, fixed set of rules.

There exists a different range of books, books that talk about the how and why of gardens, what the garden represents, and what it tries to convey. For example, the books of John Dixon Hunt, Charles Quest Ritson, Ton Lemaire, and Simon Schama all broadened my perception of what a garden is or can be. These books tell how different people have different relations to the natural world and are shaped by location, culture, and time. Take, for example, the Splice Garden that American landscape architect Martha Schwartz designed for the Whitehead Institute for Biomedical Research, a microbiology research center in Cambridge, MA. There the rooftop garden is a hybrid between a formal French garden and a Japanese rock garden. In making this "chimera," Schwartz related the garden to the research at the institute. She made the garden "a cautionary tale about the dangers inherent in gene splicing: the possibility of creating a monster."[14] The garden can be a means of communication through its design, planting, and maintenance.

I once mentioned one of my favorite garden books, *39 Haveplaner (39 Garden Plans)* by Sørensen, to a friend. In this book Sørensen draws up thirty-nine plans for the same garden, all completely different and all based on one main idea. After reading the book, my friend remarked, "I don't like it; it's not practical. I don't see how I can use this in creating a garden." These are all reasons why I love the book. It's the same with the gardens I like, it is the essays, the tests, the non-conforming books that I keep returning to. It is exactly the same reason why I keep coming back to certain gardens. The books, like the gardens, are queer; they highlight a different, often overlooked aspect, apart from the normative, mainstream approach.

To me, these books and gardens function like the avant-garde or haute couture: they don't exist to solve a problem or be practical. Instead, they seduce, they invent, they inspire. They open new ways to think about gardens, to make gardens and to be in gardens. And gardens for me seem to keep on offering new ways to understand them, as Erik Jong argues,

> [The] garden has multiple meanings. It is a place where feelings and memories may be expressed. It can reveal contested meanings and is, therefore, an important theme in art and literature. In the garden, time passes with a certain slowness, which contrasts with the acceleration of global consumer and commercial culture. This distance from the world facilitates the necessary awareness of our relationship with nature, and in particular of our surviving colonial relationship with people, animals, and plants. We can explore our own nature in the garden, our identity and gender, the meaning of our origin and birthplace, the dimensions of our social inclusion or exclusion.[15]

The line about how we can "explore our own nature in the garden," confirms why I feel certain gardens, and garden books, stick with me. Such gardens and books open "a window to the spirit"[16] for me.

MORE THAN A PASTIME

These layers of multiple meanings in gardens, and their relation to spirit, to existence itself, have resonated strongly with me. Growing up in an atheist family, with teachers as parents, I was compelled to work hard to be well behaved, have good grades, be in control of my emotions, and be on time. I know how to function and behave in normative society, but I don't have a big story that carries me through life. I lacked, as Dutch poet Gerrit Komrij would put it, "a worldview."

Growing up atheist and queer made this even more complex. Heteronormative actions, like finding a girlfriend, starting a family, going on holidays with the kids, are of course all possible, but they are less self-evident and more the result of a choice. For queer people, there's less of a blueprint for life. Instead, growing up queer offers "the potentiality of a life unscripted by the conventions of family, inheritance, and child rearing."[17] Designer and lecturer Jaffer Kolb writes about queerness as "an open mesh of possibilities, gaps, overlaps, dissonances, resonances, lapses and excesses of meaning."[18] This has an upside—the opportunity to shape your own world—but also a downside. Freed from (hetero)normative conventions and religion, questions remain: What is the big story in your/my life? If it's not religion or raising a family, then what is it?

This need for a big story, for meaning, is natural. Paul Cliteur notes, "The need for meaning is a primal human fact. We all build a worldview or philosophy of life."[19] For a long time, I've been struggling with this. What is my worldview? How can I find a way of being in this world? How can I root myself? And now, in hindsight, I see that gardens and garden literature helped me create a worldview.

Similarly, Ganzevoort and Roeland discuss gardening from within the framework of practical theology. They talk about how for many gardeners the activities of gardening "are far from trivial, but rather highly meaningful ways of being in the world" relating to "notions of sacredness, transcendence and existentiality" and how gardening can be defined as a "quasi-religion" or "para-religion."[20] They conclude that the praxis of gardening "is not mundane or insignificant, but full of spiritual meanings."[21]

The garden, for me, does have this spiritual meaning. Even though a lot of the activities in the garden seem to be rather mundane, in essence they all relate back to positioning yourself in this world, trying to harness the forces of nature, trying to please the elements in order to receive food, flowers, and peace of mind. The garden functions as an icon, an emblem for our relation to nature and a window to the spirit. I believe that was true also for Jarman, Lloyd, Carpenter, Gerritsen, and others mentioned above. The garden is more than a hobby or a pastime. It is "an existential and spiritual activity."[22]

MY OWN ALLOTMENT

Today, I have my own allotment garden. It is located on a small island in the river Maas. It's a space filled with plants, collected over the years, composed without a clear plan, growing in whatever way they like. How controlled my grandmother's garden was, how uncontrolled mine is. I'm a lazy gardener; I add some stuff and remove some stuff, but mostly let it go. I relate to the words of Jessica Andrews: "I gravitated towards the disorderly green spaces where it felt as though life was allowed to happen on its own terms."[23] I tell myself I'm doing this on purpose, to let nature have its way, to resist the normative constraints of the other allotment

Figure 5. My own allotment garden in Rotterdam, 2021. Photo by author.

gardens around mine. Maybe I am, and maybe my approach to cultivating my garden is the same as my approach to cultivating my own sense of self.

When I visit my garden, I first make a round: how is my *Thalictrum rochebreanum* doing? Is that one branch still drooping a bit? And those ferns I planted last week, are they doing okay? Or is that aggressive *Acanthus* smothering them? The garden is not slavishly waiting for my husband and me to arrive, but has a life of its own; the plants are growing, the wind is blowing, the birds are chirping, even when we have long gone home. My husband and I are in the minority: there are many more birds and insects and plants and trees. The garden belongs to them, and we blow by from time to time.

The garden is a nuisance and a joy, a lot of work and a lot of loitering about, a lot of growth and death, while offering a window to the spirit. The place provokes an abundance of dualities and triggers a range of thoughts and actions. Noticing a dead worm somewhere can let loose an avalanche of spiritual thoughts. And a philosophical thought may be interrupted by dogs barking at the wind.

The feeling I have in my own allotment is very similar to what I experienced in the garden of Kleine Oma: it is a safe haven, with its own rituals and cycles. It is a place of otherness, it is a queer space, and it is my space. As with others before me, I've made myself a place to feel safe, to feel connected, to feel a sense of belonging, to open a window to my spirit. In my allotment, I try to grow flowers, but deep down, consciously or subconsciously, I try to grow a "meaningful way of being in the world."[24] In the garden, I try to root myself in this world.

NOTES

1. Clément, *Gardens, Landscape, and Nature's Genius*, 24.
2. Naydler, *Gardening as a Sacred Art*, 9.
3. Verhagen, *Het Geluk van de Tuin*, 32.
4. Crowdy, "Queer Growth."
5. Betsky, *Queer Space*, back cover.
6. Pavka, "What Do We Mean by Queer Space?"
7. Gavroche, "Queer Desire and Revolution."
8. Pavka, "What Do We Mean by Queer Space?"
9. Crowdy, "Queer Growth."
10. Pavka, "What Do We Mean by Queer Space?"
11. Paul Cliteur uses the term "collectivistic perspective," to describe how it is human to rejoice in the knowledge that we're not the only one with this worldview, that we've found likeminded people.
12. Quoted in Quest-Ritson, *The English Garden: A Social History*, 9.
13. Gerritsen, *Buiten is het Groen*, 5.
14. Martha Schwartz Partners, "Whitehead Institute 'Splice Garden.'"
15. De Jong, Erik A., "Like a Mirror," 11–12.
16. Naydler, *Gardening as a Sacred Art*, 98.
17. Ahmed, *Queer Phenomenology*, 177.
18. Kolb, quoted in Pavka, "What do we mean by Queer Space?"
19. Cliteur, "Het begin van seculiere zingeving," 11.
20. Ganzevoort and Roeland, "Lived Religion," 94–95.
21. Ganzevoort and Roeland, "Lived Religion," 99.

22. Ganzevoort and Roeland, "Lived Religion," 92.
23. Andrews, "A woman Seeks Room in London," 43–45.
24. Ganzevoort and Roeland, "Lived Religion," 94.

REFERENCES

Andrews, Jessica. "A Woman Seeks Room in London." In *Towards Abundance: The Delightful Paradoxes of Gender*, edited by John Jennifer Marx, 41–45. London: Architectural Review, 2023.

Ahmed, Sarah. *Queer Phenomenology: Orientations, Objects, Others*. Durham, NC: Duke University Press, 2006.

Betsky, Aaron. *Queer Space: Architecture and Same-Sex Desire*. New York: William Morrow, 1997.

Clément, Gilles. *Gardens, Landscape and Nature's Genius*. Aarhus: Ikaros, 2020.

Cliteur, Paul. "Het begin van seculiere zingeving." In *Cultuur, politiek en christelijke traditie*, edited by P.B. Cliteur, 9–21. Baarn: Callenbach, 1996.

Cluitmans, Laurie. Introduction to *On the Necessity of Gardening: An ABC of Art, Botany and Cultivation*, edited by Laurie Cluitmans, 11–12. Amsterdam: Valiz, 2021.

Crowdy, Joe. "Queer Growth: Peace and Refuge in the Garden." *Architectural Review*, February 2021. https://www.architectural-review.com/essays/queer-growth-peace-and-refuge-in-the-garden.

De Jong, Erik A. "Like a Mirror." Foreword to *On the Necessity of Gardening: An ABC of Art, Botany and Cultivation*, edited by Laurie Cluitmans, 11–12. Amsterdam: Valiz, 2021.

Ganzevoort, R. Ruard, and Johan H. Roeland. "Lived Religion: The Praxis of Practical Theology." *International Journal of Public Theology* 18, no.1 (2014): 91–101.

Gavroche, Julius. "Queer Desire and Revolution." Autonomies (blog), October 5, 2018. https://autonomies.org/2018/10/queer-desire-and-revolution.

Gerritsen, Henk. *Buiten is het Groen*. Amsterdam: Architectura & Natura, 2008.

Lemaire, Ton. *Met open zinnen*. Amsterdam: Ambo, 2002.

Martha Schwartz Partners, "Whitehead Institute 'Splice Garden.'" Accessed January 29, 2024. https://msp.world/projects/whitehead-institute-splice-garden.

Mortimer-Sandilands, Catriona, and Bruce Erikson, eds. *Queer Ecologies: Sex, Nature, Politics, Desire*. Bloomington: Indiana University Press, 2010.

Naydler, Jeremy. *Gardening as a Sacred Art*. Edinburgh: Floris, 2011.

Pavka, Evan. "What Do We Mean by Queer Space?" *Azure Magazine*, June 29, 2020. https://www.azuremagazine.com/article/what-do-we-mean-by-queer-space.

Quest-Ritson, Charles. *The English Garden: A Social History*. London: Penguin, 2001.

Sørensen, Carl Theodor. *39 Haveplaner. Typiske haver til et typehus*. Copenhagen: Arkitektens, 1966.

Verhagen, Pieter. *Het Geluk van de Tuin*. Amsterdam: Gianotten, 2004.

MICHAEL KOTUTWA JOHNSON

PLANTING BY FAITH: A HOPI FARMER'S PERSPECTIVE

Since time immemorial, my people, the Hopi of northern Arizona, have been planting on what is now commonly referred to as the Colorado Plateau. The plateau only receives about six to ten inches of precipitation annually. Some may ask, "Why is this significant?" It's significant because our Hopi people raise a variety of crops such as corn, beans, and squash with low amounts of precipitation and no human-made irrigation system. I was told by crop scientists at Cornell University, where I received my undergraduate degree, that raising crops like corn would require something like thirty-three inches of precipitation.

To understand this type of semi-arid agriculture one must first ask the questions, "What makes growing crops such as corn, in a semi-arid region, possible?" and "Given the occasional crop failures that occur, why not just irrigate to guarantee a crop every year?" Let me start off by explaining what is behind our practices and why we continue to plant despite all the challenges, such as drought, that we face. The following was told to me by various Hopi elders including Harold Joseph and my grandfather, Fred Aptvi.

It was explained to me when my people first arrived in our region over two thousand years ago, we met what we refer to as the guardian of this world, who goes by the name of Massaw. He was very hesitant about our arrival because he knew of human beings and their tendency to drift toward immorality. Massaw was the caretaker of the land we wanted to live on. However, over time he agreed to allow us to live on what we call Hopi *Tutsqua* (land), but only if we agreed to be stewards of the land. He gave us specific instructions on how to live and gave us a planting stick, seed, and gourd of water as tools for survival. He also said that to live in this semi-arid region and survive we must have "faith" in everything we do.

So, even before the Hopi had ceremonies, we were farmers—farmers whose very survival was based on faith. There is no separation between our spiritual system and our agricultural system. They are interdependent and rely on each other. For example, the white corn we raise is often ground and made into corn meal that is not only eaten but also offered as a blessing and used to say prayers. When a baby is born, he or she is lifted toward the sun and has a piece of Hopi sweet corn pudding placed in his or her mouth to tie the baby to our land. During this event the child is also given a Hopi name. My name is Kotutwa, which when translated into English means, "embers like those coals seen as the fire dies down."

As Hopi we do not regard plants and the products we produce as mere commodities; they are like our children and thus nurtured throughout their life cycle. There is no economic return on the investment of Hopi agriculture; the only returns are our survival and the renewal of the covenant we made with Massaw countless generations ago. Our agriculture is faith-driven.

For example, in the spring of 2018, I realized that I was probably not going to have a crop because I did not see the plants I usually see during that time of the year, which is near our planting season. That spring, after meeting with other Hopi farmers, I decided to only plant about an eighth of my fields. The corn seeds lay dormant in the ground from the beginning of planting season (which for me is about the beginning of May) until the first significant rainfall, which occurred in the first week of August that year. Two weeks later, I went walking in my field and saw my children (corn plants) emerging from their mother (earth) to catch the first rays of sunlight. If I did not have faith—I saw some Hopi farmers choose not to plant because of the drought—I would not have seen my children come up after what I call a long and much-needed sleep. I was able to harvest fresh corn that October and had enough to give to Hopi people I knew. It was not just about a renewal of my crops emerging; it was also about a renewal of my faith and thus my spirituality. I often tell this story not for the benefit of listening to my own voice but rather to spread the message of hope.

Our agricultural system is place-based. As a result, we have become familiar with our vegetation that determines how deep the soil moisture is, as certain plants' rooting systems vary. If we see an abundance of plants with shallow roots turning green, we do not have to plant very deep. Hopi corn is planted anywhere from six to eighteen inches deep, depending on the depth of moisture in the soil. Usually, ten to fifteen kernels are placed in a single hole. The holes are spaced about three paces, or six feet, apart from each other. All the techniques of the Hopi are designed to preserve soil moisture.

Raising a field requires a lot of work in the environment that defines Hopi *Tutsqua*, and it is only through our connectedness to our plants and ceremonies that it is still practiced at Hopi. Planting at Hopi is spiritual, not just an exercise or practice. It is regenerative in so many ways that it carries a tremendous number of values.

Today, as a practitioner of Hopi agriculture and an Assistant Professor at the University of Arizona's School of Natural Resources and the Environment and Indigenous Resilience Center, I often hear the term "regenerative agriculture." Regenerative agriculture is the holistic practice of managing an agricultural system to improve and preserve soil fertility. Some have given credit to Indigenous people for having practiced regenerative agriculture since time immemorial.

However, one would be hard pressed to find a definition accurately encompassing our unique view of why we manage the place-based agriculture systems that have ensured our survival. So, if credit is given to Indigenous people for such a term as "regenerative agriculture," should not our value systems and cultural beliefs also be a part of the definition? I came up with the following definition of what I term Indigenous regenerative agriculture. It reads as follows:

> Indigenous regenerative agriculture is the process of incorporating Indigenous place-based ways of knowing and land use management schemes adapted for survival that are supported by culture, belief systems, and community, incorporated over a millennium.

You see, it is not just the planting of crops that makes Indigenous agricultural systems unique; in some ways, it is the resilience of these systems that must be stressed. The amount of nurturing for our crops that takes place on Hopi *Tutsqua* should not be lost or forgotten. The key to equity for Indigenous people is not new programs that will help resolve their socio-economic issues, but rather recognition and enhancement of our cultural value systems.

It is no coincidence that eighty percent of the world's biodiversity is now found on only twenty percent of the land and in the hands of a mere five percent of the population. In this case, the five percent are Indigenous societies. The question should be asked: What happened to the biodiversity that is not controlled by the non-Indigenous population?

Biodiversity and natural resources in general are deemed to be responsible for over half of the world's gross domestic product (GDP). One would think that the management of such high rates of biodiversity would make Indigenous people rich, but unfortunately this is not the case.

I may have found an answer to the question, but I did not realize it until I was drafting this essay. When I was a young child, about ten years old, my father would drop me off at my grandfather's house on the Hopi reservation sometime during the summer. I remember that one time, we went to gather a plant he wanted to find, as he said it would help him with his eyesight. We walked a long way to find that plant. Once we found it, I bent over to pick it up. My grandfather told me, "No, leave it; we will get the next one." He said that this one is for the next person to find.

You see, it's not just about the extraction of resources, such as the rare plant I just described; it's about leaving something behind for someone else. It's our faith and cultural belief system at Hopi, and the covenant we made with Massaw, that is important. It's this cultural belief system that has been ingrained in us as Hopi to be true stewards of the land. It's not about our economic well-being but rather our spiritual well-being, which has no monetary cost associated with it. Agriculture at Hopi is about so much more than just raising plants: it's about raising people.

Hopi agriculture and the Hopi farmers who have farmed in the semi-arid Southwest for millennia have faced constant environmental and personal challenges. However, many of us are still fulfilling our obligations and honoring our covenant. We are reminded of this when we look at a small ear of Hopi blue corn, as it represents humility, patience, and endurance. All of these qualities are needed to ensure the prosperity of the next generation of Hopi people—if not humanity.

I titled this essay, "Planting by Faith: A Hopi Farmers Perspective." I have offered my perspective in this essay and told you a few stories along the way. The *Novati* (knowledge) I pass along is not mine alone but has been passed down to me by my grandfather and others who shared their insights with me. In many ways I am like the same crops I raise. I have been "Planted by Faith."

MEGHANN ORMOND

UNSETTLED: ON LEARNING TO HONOR POWERFUL STRANGERS IN AN "IMMIGRANT WORLD"

> Wherever you are is called Here,
> And you must treat it as a powerful stranger,
> Must ask permission to know it and be known.
> —David Wagoner, "Lost."[1]

Slipping out of the pickup truck and, to my grandmother's chagrin, out of my shoes, my bare feet settle into the moist black earth of the vegetable patch at the back of our Wapakoneta farm in northwestern Ohio. Refreshed by the soil, the evening light, and the first cool breeze since morning, as we weed and water the plants, I look around and slowly take in all that is precious in my young world. My grandparents, perpetually in motion, weave quietly between beets, string beans, sweetcorn, tomatoes, and the vines of cucumbers and pumpkins that we'll eat fresh or can for later. In the buckeye tree at the edge of the nearby woods, eye-shaped leaves screen discreet birds relaxedly cooing as the day unwinds. To our backs, the tall windmill lazily turns to harness fresh groundwater and escort it into the cattail-ringed pond with its plump bass and bluegill.

This landscape is what first comes to me when I conjure up the word "home."

Our vegetable patch sits at some distance from the house and the agricultural land used for intensive soybean and corn production. During the deep spring plough of those adjacent fields, my grandfather routinely unearths, and comes to fill the kitchen drawer next to the refrigerator with, flint arrowheads. In between helping my grandparents with the gardening, I try to find one myself, to be able to feel it light in my hand and touch its sharp edges chipped by the Indigenous peoples that had first felt at home on this land. But, try as I might to find a smoky grey point jutting out of the ground in our vegetable patch, I am invariably greeted instead by confused earthworms struggling to make sense of the daylight to which my poking around has exposed them.

The only arrowheads I ever manage to find are those stowed away in the kitchen drawer. It turns out that only years of deep machine tilling—not the hoes and trowels we'd use to lightly turn the soil in our little vegetable patch—could excavate those arrowheads from their ancient wooded marshland resting places.[2]

Decades later and an ocean away, I show my six-year-old son one of the arrowheads from my grandfather's collection—it's among the few items that accompanied me in my migration to Europe. He demonstrates polite interest for a few seconds, touching it delicately, then returns to his Legos in our Utrecht apartment, the only home he knows. He has not yet set foot on the land cultivated by my settler ancestors and, since the land was partly sold off when my grandfather passed away, he may never be able to. Alas, this ancient artifact—something I dreamed of finding at his age—can be used neither to build what now matters to him nor connect him to what matters to me. Like migrants throughout the ages, I need to find another way to convey something to my child about where I come from and why it matters.

I have lived in apartments in densely populated European cities for more than half of my life now. With no chance to cultivate and create ties with the soil, I have long felt like a squatter—at best a perpetual guest, at worst a parasite. Weary from this, I gifted myself the use of a small community garden plot in Utrecht a few years back. In the spring and summer months, I've again got the dirty fingernails I had as a child; these are now accompanied by the calloused hands, aching shoulders, and cracking knees of an adult working with the soil. Preparing the soil, spreading seed, transplanting seedlings, watering, weeding, composting, watering some more, weeding some more, composting some more, my body moves in the unassuming rhythms and forms I recall as intimately familiar to my grandparents. Through this embodied practice, I realize that I come closest to the first moment I can recall feeling at home in the world. And the realization of this brings both deep surprise and relief.

AN IMMIGRANT'S HOME/LAND?

If home for me is not located in a particular location—a specific plot of land with cadastral co-ordinates—but rather an attuned practice grounding me in the "Here,"[3] then perhaps I can share it with my son because it also moves with me. This realization makes me alert to my responsibility to not only convey to him the deep joy of connecting with the aliveness of the land[4]—wherever that might be in the world—but also to better understand the more-than-human entwinements out of which this practice I so deeply value has grown.

As someone with a background of multi-generational migration—having not only migrated from the United States to Europe but also being the descendent of colonial settlers that migrated from all over Europe to the United States—I am increasingly preoccupied with how to constructively "stay with the trouble"[5] of this "immigrant world"[6] of disconnection and alienation in which my—and countless others'—relationship to land is refracted through notions of severance, stunting, and fragmentation—a prism re-imagined and multiplied by the centuries-long workings of colonial capitalism.

In light of this, I've been mulling over two passages that address immigration in Potawatomi field biologist Robin Wall Kimmerer's 2013 book, *Braiding Sweetgrass*, which draws from a pre-Columbian cosmology shared by many Indigenous peoples originally from around the Great Lakes region of the land today recognized as part of the United States and Canada to offer teachings from the land in this era of profound environmental crisis.[7] In one passage, she notes that, upon their creation out of the four sacred elements, humans were introduced into an ancient land already fully peopled by more-than-human beings. First Man (Nanabozho), therefore, was—in her words—an "immigrant" learning to integrate:

> With all the power and all the failings of a human being, Nanabozho did his best with the Original Instructions and tried to become native to his new home. His legacy is that we are still trying. But the instructions have gotten tattered along the way and many have been forgotten.[8]

Yet, while acknowledging that all humans are relative newcomers from the perspective of the more-than-human world, Kimmerer suggests in the next passage that, by carefully heeding and learning from the land's original more-than-human inhabitants, Indigenous peoples—descendants of "First Man"—did a better job at integrating than those she refers to as "Second Man." "Second Man" is understood here to include all those who, like me and my ancestors, migrated within the human-made framework of colonial capitalism that exploits through appropriation both human and more-than-human beings alike. She writes:

I want to envision a way that an immigrant society could become Indigenous to place, but I'm stumbling on the words. Immigrants cannot by definition be Indigenous. . . . .No amount of time or caring changes history or substitutes for soul-deep fusion with the land. Following [the First Man] Nanabozho's footsteps doesn't guarantee transformation of Second Man to First. But if people do not feel "Indigenous," can they nevertheless enter into the deep reciprocity that renews the world? Is this something that can be learned? Where are the teachers? I'm remembering the words of elder Henry Linkers. "You know, they came here thinking they'd get rich by working on the land. So, they dug their mines and cut down the trees. But the land is the one with the power—while they were working on the land, the land was working on them. Teaching them."[9]

As a young child, I was sometimes told that our vegetable patch at the back of the family farm back in Ohio was on "virgin" land. I had no idea of the colonial connotations of that term at the time[10]—I only understood that it denoted something special to my grandparents, distinct from the big fields that yielded the arrowhead I shared with my son. Spared from intensive cash crop cultivation by five generations of my settler ancestors, this garden plot did not need to rely on the chemical fertilizers and pesticides or the drainage ditches that the cash crop agriculture in the other fields required. The soil in our vegetable patch had not been subjected to deadening appropriation under the singular terms of capital accumulation—it was, well, still alive in rich complexity. And it worked with us to produce food that neither resembled nor tasted anything like the bleak industrialized produce one could find on the shelves of an average chain supermarket in the early 1980s. I want my son to know why. Perhaps, in recognizing and learning from the "powerful stranger" in my childhood "Here," we may both be more capable of honoring our current "Here" as one as well.[11]

INDIGENOUS LANDS

In the time before Europeans explored and settled the area, the land on which our vegetable patch was located was part of the extensive wooded marshland that European settlers later came to call the "Great Black Swamp."[12] Legend holds that "the forest was so thick that a squirrel could travel from the Ohio River to Lake Erie without ever touching ground."[13] The walnut, hickory, ash, and elm provided habitat for deer, elk, wolf, cougar, badger, beaver, bear, and muskrat—ideal hunting grounds for Indigenous peoples over millennia. At the invitation of the Miami people that used this area as their seasonal hunting grounds, many Shawnee came to settle here by the seventeenth century. European trade, disease, and westward colonial expansion had displaced the Shawnee people from their ancestral, pre-contact homeland.[14] The Great Black Swamp became home to the largest and most prominent Shawnee settlement in the territory of the "Old Northwest" and what later became the state of Ohio.

The Shawnee—like their contemporaries from other communities—lived in semi-permanent settlements in spring and summer, with women in charge of subsistence agriculture and, in autumn and winter, they would turn to the forest for sustenance, with men going on hunting expeditions and women gathering nuts and berries. Corn, beans, and squash—the Three Sisters—were the staple foods, traditionally planted together to symbiotically nourish and protect one another and the soil.[15] Visiting the Shawnee here in 1813, a U.S. soldier noticed a profusion of "vines, such as pumpkins, water and muskmelons, cucumbers, beans of various kinds, growing among their corn which was planted without any kind of order"[16] being tended by women.

He was not alone in being struck by the contrast between "disorderly" Shawnee and "orderly" American settler agricultural practices and by the absence of cash crops, fruit trees, or livestock. Facing growing pressure to show white American authorities they could live like "civilized" settlers in order to be able to stay on this land, the Shawnee people here, under the guidance of Quaker missionaries, began adopting "the agrarian values on which most American men obsessed"[17] by shifting men away from hunting toward cultivating cash crops and "freeing up" women from engaging in subsistence agriculture to "run the home" like their settler counterparts.[18] Agricultural "civilizing" meant taming Shawnee people into laboring bodies serving the emerging needs of white American agroindustry in a part of the country where slavery had been outlawed.[19] Ultimately, the U.S. government did force the Shawnee to surrender their remaining territory and, in 1832, as a consequence of Jackson's Indian Removal Act, they were again uprooted by the expansion of colonial capitalism, this time forcibly relocated to new reservations west of the Mississippi River with landscapes and conditions very unlike those to which they were accustomed.[20]

My settler ancestors—part of the great stream of Catholic Saxon, Hessian, and Alsatian day laborers fleeing poverty and the inability to hold rights to or afford land of their own, lured by the promise of inexpensive farmland in the United States—were among the first European "pioneers" in an area newly voided of Indigenous peoples. They purchased one hundred square acres of land that only a few years prior had been the heart of a Shawnee reservation.[21] Their plot in the grid (see "Kreitzer" in the bottom center-right of Figure 1) reflects the "formal systems—colonial, military, and fiscal—that alchemized the lands of an Indian continent [...] into an abstraction, and thus a commodity ripe for speculation."[22] Land taken from the First People and sold to Second People—yeomen like my ancestors—enabled the U.S. government to pay off its Revolutionary War debt.[23]

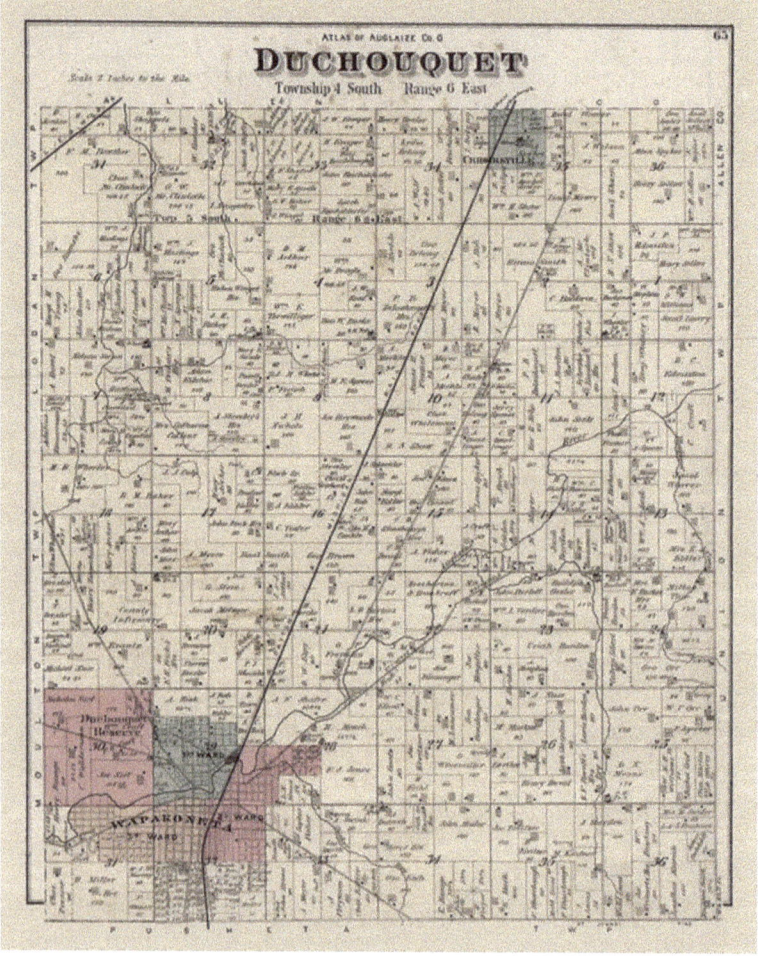

Figure 1. Duchouquet Township, Auglaize County, Ohio.[24]

For these yeomen, who did not need to be inculcated in market-rationalized agricultural practices, the new plots' terrains constituted a formidable "obstacle to be conquered."[25] They spent their first decades turning the newly American landscape they were settling into one akin to that of their land of origin, recreating what they understood to be land suitable for cash crop agriculture by clearing the dense forest and draining the marshland into ditches.[26] Fleischhauer writes,

> A visitor to this part of Ohio is struck by the similarity of the landscape; flat country with a wide horizon and a tremendous sky above it, farmhouses with large, prosperous barns and groves of oak trees and other hardwood. In any direction, before one becomes aware of a town, one sees the stately church towers rising from the plain. The swamps that covered large tracts of land when the first immigrants arrived, have disappeared, reclaimed into fertile fields as have those in the pioneers' native Westphalia and Lower Saxony. The early settlers must have felt at home here.[27]

Within only a couple of generations, a millennia-old landscape had been completely transformed by an "immigrant world"[28] desperate to bring familiar order to that which was unfamiliar. The farming-based "German villages" that came to flourish in the area—with Catholic, Lutheran, Calvinist (German Reformed), and Anabaptist (Amish and Mennonite) settlements set up along kinship and religious divides—simply replicated what they knew.

DECOLONIZING THE LAND TODAY

By the early 1980s, when I spent time in the vegetable patch, some 150 years had passed since the last Shawnee had left, and we were five generations deep into ever-more-intense technoscientific agricultural practices leading to dangerous algae blooms, much reduced biodiversity, and increased cancer rates in the human population. Besides the occasional arrowhead, there were very few traces left of the area's pre-settler heritage in the landscape. Everyone sped past the weathered roadside heritage markers that spoke of battles, treaties, and settlements,[29] and no one knew the meaning of our town's Shawnee name, Wapakoneta. Outside of those arrowheads that turned up every once in a while, other hints of the pre-settler heritage of the area, such as the local "Wigwam,"[30] where my mother regularly did Jazzercize, and the "Thunderbirds"[31] Catholic school mascot from the nearby city of Lima, had been appropriated and given new meaning to serve settler community interests. The Three Sisters, now separated from one another to grow in orderly rows, were reserved for Thanksgiving Day tales and seasonal porch decorations, their significance to most being overshadowed by the cheap, plentiful food available at the local air-conditioned supermarket.

Yet, less obvious traces of the area's pre-settler heritage did persist in the land itself. Our vegetable patch, still teeming with life, was made possible by centuries of non-invasive cultivation practices and the rich soils of the thick forest that once covered this plot. As someone deeply implicated in the violence wrought by the heavily extractive settler-colonial social and agricultural practices that sustained generations of my family with food, shelter, and a steady income, the deep affection my grandparents and I had for—and indeed, the reverential entanglement with—this particular plot of land, this "powerful stranger,"[32] stirs up great ambivalence and leaves me thoroughly unsettled.

The passages from Kimmerer's *Braiding Sweetgrass* on immigration and indigeneity that I shared earlier remind me of the challenge of both heeding the wisdom of Indigenous knowledges and avoiding the "nostalgic" salvaging of those diverse knowledges to redeem ourselves from the colonial violence for which my and others' settler ancestors are responsible for initiating, and for which I and contemporary others are implicated in perpetuating, on Indigenous and enslaved peoples as well as more-than-human beings.[33] There is no redemption for the past. There is only embracing responsibility and potential for the present and the future.

Decolonizing environmental allyship, argues Kyle Powys Whyte, requires us to recognize the ways in which we "are living in the environmental fantasies of [our] settler ancestors" and to change them while not perpetuating "romantic stereotypes or symbols of a common humanity."[34] I don't wish to be lulled into the false possibility that somehow I could "become indigenous 'again.'"[35] In this "immigrant world,"[36] I am decidedly not indigenous anywhere to anyone, but potentially planet Earth itself. Because of this, I seek to heed the call that Kimmerer and others are making for us to pay attention to the reciprocal ways in which we work with and on the land,[37] and the land works with and on us in order "to open up for new assemblages that generate metamorphic transformation in our capacity to affect and be affected—and also to feel, think, and imagine."[38]

Over this past year, we've said goodbye to the Utrecht community garden plot and hello to a small backyard in the Dutch university town of

Wageningen. You can find me there, puttering about nearly every day among the berries, apples, cabbages, carrots, squash, beans, and corn we've planted—barefoot whenever possible. Our energy goes not only into growing fruits and vegetables but also into supporting the recovery of the soil, impoverished by the upheaval of recent construction in the area. Between the beds, the compost bin—regularly nourished by fermented food scraps and other organic material—is home to all sorts of bacteria, worms, woodlice, and snails. Teeming and teaming with past and present more-than-human life, soil, Puig de la Bellacasa reminds us, is the source of life and regeneration.[39] Through consciously caring together for the soil, my son and I are learning how to better honor this "powerful stranger"—this wise teacher—in our joint "Here."[40] It is a "homing" practice that has inspired me to develop a deeper awareness and appreciation of the more-than-human assemblages across time and space that underpin the affective earthly attachments and heritage practices I wish to pass on to my son.[41]

ACKNOWLEDGEMENTS

The author would like to thank the anonymous reviewers, Johan Roeland and Edward Huijbens for their nuanced reflections that helped to sharpen the final version of this text.

NOTES

1. Wagoner, "Lost," 219.
2. Given their shape and material, the arrowheads were likely used by the Adena or Hopewell peoples during the late Archaic to middle Woodland period somewhere between 500 BCE and 500 CE. See Chidester, "Re-evaluating Colonization and Cultural Change" and Hothem, "Native American Artifacts: Arrowheads."
3. Wagoner, "Lost," 219.
4. See Turner, "Embodied Connections."
5. Haraway, *Staying with the Trouble*.
6. Kimmerer, *Braiding Sweetgrass*, 264.
7. Kimmerer, *Braiding Sweetgrass*, 264.
8. Kimmerer, *Braiding Sweetgrass*, 205–7.
9. Kimmerer, *Braiding Sweetgrass*, 213.
10. Van der Marel, "Unsettling *North of Summer*."
11. Wagoner, "Lost," 219.
12. Levy, "Learning to Love the Great Black Swamp."
13. USDA, "Early Settlement."

14. Walton, "The Forgotten History of Ohio's Indigenous Peoples"; Brown, et al., "The Shawnee."
15. Warren, "The Ohio Shawnees' Struggle Against Removal," 43; Kimmerer, *Braiding Sweetgrass*.
16. Schillinger, in Warren, "The Ohio Shawnees' Struggle Against Removal," 43.
17. Warren, "The Ohio Shawnees' Struggle Against Removal," 44.
18. Warren, "The Ohio Shawnees' Struggle Against Removal," 78.
19. Warren, "The Ohio Shawnees' Struggle Against Removal."
20. Warren, "The Ohio Shawnees' Struggle Against Removal"; Kimmerer, *Braiding Sweetgrass*.
21. *Wapakoneta Republican*, Unknown Title [Obituary for Mrs. Jacob Kreitzer].
22. Deloria, "What Tecumseh Fought For."
23. Deloria, "What Tecumseh Fought For."
24. Howland, "Duchouquet Township, Auglaize County, Ohio."
25. USDA, "Early Settlement."
26. *Wapakoneta Republican*, "Death Takes Well Known Citizen Sunday"; Levy, "Learning to Love the Great Black Swamp."
27. Fleischhauer, "German Communities in Northwestern Ohio."
28. Kimmerer, *Braiding Sweetgrass*, 264.
29. See, e.g., Irick, "Wapaghonetta Reservation: The Shawnee Reservation at Wapakoneta - The Eastern Boundary Marker."
30. A Shawnee semi-permanent domed dwelling made of tree bark and used in summer.
31. The Shawnee spirits of war that guard the entrance to heaven, responsible for stirring up storms, with lightning issued from their blinking eyes and thunder from their collisions with evil creatures.
32. Wagoner, "Lost," 219.
33. Whyte, "White Allies"; Phillips, *Staging Indigeneity*; Tuck and Yang, "Decolonization is Not a Metaphor."
34. Whyte, "White Allies."
35. Puig de la Bellacasa, "Re-animating Soils," 402.
36. Kimmerer, *Braiding Sweetgrass*.
37. Kimmerer, *Braiding Sweetgrass*; Stengers, "Reclaiming Animism"; Puig de la Bellacasa, "Re-animating Soils."
38. Stengers, "Reclaiming Animism," para. 60.
39. Puig de la Bellacasa, "Re-animating Soils"; Verkerk, *Onder het Maaiveld*.
40. Wagoner, "Lost," 219.
41. Ter Kuile, *The Power of Ritual*; Huijbens, *Developing Earthly Attachments in the Anthropocene*.

REFERENCES

Brown, Sally, Joe Stahlman, Bonnie M. Brown, Beth Toren, and Michael Sherwin. "The Shawnee." *Indigenous Appalachia*, West Virginia University, Fall 2022. https://researchrepository.wvu.edu/cgi/viewcontent. cgi?article=1024&context=indigenous exhibit#:~:text=Thus%2C%20the%20 Shawnee%20are%20often,the%20greater%20Ohio%20River%20region

Chidester, Robert C. "Re-evaluating Colonization and Cultural Change During the Early Archaic Period in Northwestern Ohio." *Archaeology of Eastern North America* 39 (2011): 109–30. https://www.jstor.org/stable/23265117

Deloria, Philip. "What Tecumseh Fought For," *New Yorker*, November 2, 2020. https://www.newyorker.com/magazine/2020/11/02/what-tecumseh-fought-for.

Fleischhauer, Wolfgang. "German Communities in Northwestern Ohio: Canal Fever and Prosperity." Society for the History of the Germans in Maryland, 1970. https://loyolanotredamelib.org/php/report05/articles/pdfs/Report34Fleischhauerp23-34.pdf

Haraway, Donna J. *Staying with the Trouble: Making Kin in the Chthulucene*. Durham, NC: Duke University Press, 2016.

Hothem, Paul. "Native American Artifacts: Arrowheads." CFAES Project Idea Starter, The Ohio State University, 2014. https://ohio4h.org/sites/ohio4h/files/imce/books_resources/Self-Determined/e365-04%20Arrowheads.pdf

Howland, H.G. "Duchouquet Township, Auglaize County, Ohio." David Rumsey Historical Map Collection, Auglaize County Historical Society, Ohio, 1880.

Huijbens, Edward H. *Developing Earthly Attachments in the Anthropocene*. London: Routledge, 2021.

Irick, Ronald. "Wapaghonetta Reservation: The Shawnee Reservation at Wapakoneta - The Eastern Boundary Marker." The Historical Marker Database, 2014. https://www.hmdb.org/m.asp?m=75195

Kimmerer, Robin Wall. *Braiding Sweetgrass: Indigenous Wisdom, Scientific Knowledge, and the Teachings of Plants*. Minneapolis: Milkweed, 2013.

Levy, Sharon. "Learning to Love the Great Black Swamp," *Undark*, March 31, 2017. https://undark.org/2017/03/31/great-black-swamp-ohio-toledo/

Phillips, Katrina. *Staging Indigeneity: Salvage Tourism and the Performance of Native American History*. Chapel Hill: University of North Carolina Press, 2021.

Puig de la Bellacasa, María. "Re-animating Soils: Transforming Human–Soil Affections Through Science, Culture and Community." *The Sociological Review* 67, no. 2 (2019): 391–407.

Stengers, Isabelle. "Reclaiming Animism." *e-flux Journal* 36 (July 2012). https://www.e-flux.com/journal/36/61245/reclaiming-animism/

Ter Kuile, Casper. *The Power of Ritual: Turning Everyday Activities into Soulful Practices*. New York: HarperCollins, 2020.

Tuck, Eve, and K. Wayne Yang. "Decolonization is Not a Metaphor." *Tabula Rasa* 38 (2012): 61–111.

Turner, Bethaney. "Embodied Connections: Sustainability, Food Systems and Community Gardens." *Local Environment* 16, no. 6 (2011): 509–22.

United States Department of Agriculture. "Early Settlement." Wayne National Forest, accessed January 29, 2024. https://www.fs.usda.gov/detail/wayne/learning/history-culture/?cid=fsm9_006138

Van der Marel, L. Camille. "Unsettling *North of Summer*: Anxieties of Ownership in the Politics and Poetics of the Canadian North." *ariel: A Review of International English Literature* 44, no. 4 (2013): 13–47.

Verkerk, Mark (dir.). *Onder het Maaiveld* M&N Media Group and EMS FILMS, 2022.

Wagoner, David. "Lost." *Poetry Magazine*, July 1971.

Walton, Jessie. "The Forgotten History of Ohio's Indigenous Peoples," *Midstory*, July 16, 2020. https://www.midstory.org/the-forgotten-history-of-ohios-indigenous-peoples/

Wapakoneta Republican. Unknown Title [Obituary for Mrs. Jacob Kreitzer], 1882.

———. "Death Takes Well Known Citizen Sunday," 1924.

Warren, Stephen. "The Ohio Shawnees' Struggle Against Removal, 1814–30." In *Enduring Nations: Native Americans in the Midwest*, edited by R. David Edmunds, 72–93. Champaign: University of Illinois Press, 2008.

Whyte, Kyle Powys. "White Allies, Let's Be Honest About Decolonization," *Yes! Magazine*, April 3, 2018. https://www.yesmagazine.org/issue/decolonize/2018/04/03/white-allies-lets-be-honest-about-decolonization

JON PAHL

TERRA-THERAPY OR, GROWING DEEP PEACE

For the past decade or so, I've managed to stay out of the asylum and, for the most part, avoid not paying a pharmaceutical company, by practicing what I've taken to calling "terra-therapy": gardening.

I'm actually lousy at it. Oh, I grow things. Last year's garden had five different kinds of basil—lemon, Thai, purple, sweet, and giant leaf (my new favorite). We had four harvests from twenty-four basil plants altogether. My wife Lisa and I make lots of pesto to freeze—a little summer in the middle of a Wisconsin winter!

And I grow potatoes, always potatoes. Among my earliest memories, around kindergarten, was harvesting potatoes on my maternal great-grandparents Oscar and Hilda Olsen's farm in rural east-central Wisconsin. They had a wooden wheelbarrow that Oscar had made, and I remember the sound the wooden wheel made as it bounced down the stone steps into their root cellar. I can also recall to this day the smell of that cellar: damp, dank, dirty, and delightful. (I also still have and use the hoe Oscar made for Hilda in his blacksmith shop—which would put it at perhaps one-hundred and sixteen years old, since they were married in 1907).

And that hoe is a gift from my father, Fred Pahl, who died last January at age 90. He began using it after Hilda died in 1972. My dad loved weeding. I miss him dearly and not only, of course, for his skill at weed eradication. My dad and I would plant potatoes together in the spring, ever since I moved back to Wisconsin (where I grew up) from Philadelphia (where I teach) in 2017. In the last couple of years, he just held the hose and watered, while I dug and kneeled and planted the Yukon Golds, and Norland Reds, and Vikings, and Russets. Our soil is sandy (we live beside a lake), and the spuds love it.

Now, those kinds of associations—improvisations, really—are the central benefit of terra-therapy. I've never received any blazing insight or dramatic conversion. But I've grown (pun intended) to appreciate that, by digging and planting in the soil, being patient, tending seedlings with care, and harvesting whatever comes up, I can experience what I call "deep peace," which is also what I think our historic religious traditions offer to us, at their best. So, in what follows, I'll describe for you my lousy gardening practices, while also drawing some help from a few other fellow travelers on the way to growing deep peace.

DEEP PEACE,[1] GARDENING, AND TRUST

I've come up with the category of "deep peace" to describe how our religious traditions aren't like economic or political institutions in their focus on accumulating, strategizing about, or organizing power. Of course, religious actors are economically and politically engaged, too. But at root (pun intended—last time, I promise!), our religious traditions have endured for millennia because they foster trust. They contribute to peace organically, so to speak, through slow and patient (and sometimes senseless) discourses, practices, communities, and institutions of many and diverse dynamics.[2] But at their core, I'm willing to wager that our religious traditions endure because they teach us to trust the Universe (and/or God, maybe), ourselves, and each other.

Now, what I've been learning over the past decade or so of avid gardening (I converted late in life) is that trust is crucial to gardening, too. I'm not a reader of gardening manuals or magazines, and I don't listen to gardening podcasts or radio shows. I'm not opposed to them: I simply don't have (or make) time.

Every spring, in other words, I take a leap of faith into the soil. I buy seeds pretty much at random, supplementing what I generate in our small greenhouse with plants from local growers. We have several Amish farms nearby that provide great organic seedlings. I don't know how best to lay out my rows. I *have* learned to put the basil in front of the tomatoes, on the south-facing side, so the tomatoes don't block the sun. And I can't dig a straight furrow to save my life. I don't really care. I never know exactly what I'm going to plant from one season to the next, and I don't spend a lot of time worrying about it. In this case, the joy is in the doing and the trusting that something good will happen.

Gardening, I've found, generates what psychologist Mihaly Csikszentmihalyi dubbed "flow."[3] You lose yourself, and find yourself, in the process of trusting that your hands will dig where needed, that you'll place the plant carefully and tuck it in, that the water will flow where you direct it, that you might have to fertilize or feed it (not too much), and that good results will come and you'll be able to enjoy a harvest. If that's not a liturgy, then I don't know what is.

LEARNING IN TWO MODES: WHAT PLANTS TEACH, WHAT WE DO

One book I did read that had something to do with gardening, at least, was Robin Wall Kimmerer's *Braiding Sweetgrass: Indigenous Wisdom, Scientific Knowledge and the Teachings of Plants*.[4] In her beautiful collection of essays, Kimmerer draws deeply from both Potawatomi tradition and her doctorate in botany to help readers learn from plants about how better to care for the world.

Near the beginning of the book, she describes making maple syrup with her daughters: "the syrup we pour over pancakes on a winter morning is summer sunshine flowing in golden streams to pool on our plates." But the sun is not just a hot ball of gas burning in the sky. No, for Potawatomi, as for many practitioners of Indigenous traditions, the sun is animate, a living being along with all rocks and birds and plants. Kimmerer coins the phrase "animacy" to describe this vibrancy woven into the heart of creation—this Spirit, as the term implies.

But making maple syrup doesn't just happen. Yes, the sap will run in the maples at just the right time. There are sun-sensors in every bud and leaf, communicating with the roots (and other trees nearby) to be alert to get the fluid going. Plants communicate with each other. But they live with us, too, and to draw from them their bounty takes labor. Kimmerer puts it like this:

> Nanabozho [the Great Spirit and Trickster] made certain that the work would never be too easy. His teachings remind us that one half of the truth is that the earth endows us with great gifts, the other half is that the gift is not enough. The responsibility does not lie with the maples alone. The other half belongs to us; we participate in its transformation. It is our work, and our gratitude, that distills the sweetness.[5]

In any garden, there's a perpetual tension—a balance, at best—between art and science, the aesthetic and the ethical, what plants can teach, and what we can do. And when I get that balance right, I discover a kind of power that grounds me. When I find that flow, I experience a power that helps me to endure the inevitable suffering of life, even the agony of grief.

But that experience of balance can be rare. Take weeding. I don't enjoy it like my dad did, but I begin every garden with a zeal to clear space for my plant babies and give them the best chance to grow. As summer turns toward fall, alas, I grow increasingly lax; basically, I let things go. I don't so much choose to do this as it just happens. The weeds win. Their victory saves me labor, but it also means that by the end of the season my haphazard rows of arugula and beans and eggplant are on their way to reverting to prairie.

The seeds have done their work, and I've taken the harvest (albeit not as much as I might have, were I a better weeder). There's a balance between what the plants do and what I do—both are necessary to achieve purpose.

And that's the power of gardening. Too much human energy has been spent extracting from and dominating nature. People tend to think of power like that as power-over, as domination.

But I've learned from my garden a lesson we all need to learn about the nature of power. Hannah Arendt taught me first that power is the capacity "to act in concert."[6] That is, power isn't force. Force and violence destroy power, often in efforts to assert it. And it was Martin Luther King, Jr. who clinched for me this way to recognize what true power is. For King, building on Arendt, power is the capacity to act in concert *"to achieve purpose."*[7]

And in gardening, we act in concert with plants to achieve their purpose—and ours. That's power. You could call it the power of love, I suppose, but that may veer too far toward the romantic. When we garden, we learn in two modes: what plants teach and what we can do. Or, as Kimmerer puts it, "Gardens are simultaneously a material and a spiritual undertaking."[8]

GARDENING AS NONVIOLENT PRACTICE: PLANTING AS PRAYER

The practices of our historic religious traditions are ways to train our brains for sociability. They are practices in nonviolence. Prayer, pilgrimage, chanting, music, dance, and other rituals are ways to move beyond instinctive fight-flight-freeze reactions into something discernibly human and communal, something linguistic-cultural. That's how I put it in *Empire of Sacrifice: The Religious Origins of American Violence*.[9]

The other side of that assertion is that I'm not naïve about how wrong our religious traditions can go nor how wrong they have gone. They are as potentially destructive as any human agencies.

And yet by both aesthetic and ethical markers, our historic traditions have batted well above the human average, I'm willing to argue. Visit the Taoist-inspired Chinese Garden of Friendship in Sydney, Australia, as I did a few years ago, where I was moved to tears. Imagine paradise as a garden, as many religious traditions do, notably Islam and Christianity. Study the teachings of the late Rabbi Jonathan Sacks; the Nobel Peace Prize laureate, activist, and Lutheran Leymah Gbowee; or the slandered Islamic preacher Fethullah Gülen, a biography of whom I published several years ago.[10]

Such pilgrimages, imagination, and study show how religious traditions can foster, through dedicated practices, habits of mind and relationships that evince what the twelfth-century German theologian Hildegard of Bingen called *viriditas*—greening power. In the garden, in other words, planting is prayer. *Viriditas*, according to Hildegard is "the lush green of life in all nature's creations as well as the healing powers of the organism. . .and the vitality of the spirit." There's plenty of that in any garden. But Hildegard did not reduce that greening power to mere material relations. "There is a power in eternity," she also wrote, "and it is green."[11]

A recent story in the *New Yorker* profiled Hildegard and her notion of *viriditas*.[12] The author, Alex Ross, focused more on Hildegard's music than on gardening, but we can extrapolate. Ross writes, "Nothing in Hildegard's philosophy is more pertinent to our wounded planet than her concept of *viriditas*—greenness, verdancy, fecundity. She almost always associates the term with the female body, especially with the womb, and it counterbalances the violence of male sexuality. At the same time, it is the primary medium of God's power on earth."[13] That is so.

Ross goes on, "Hildegard's final theological testament, *Book of Divine Works*, begins with a vision of Caritas, the spirit of Divine Love, who, clad in a robe as bright as the sun, speaks as nature incarnate." We might imagine her standing in a garden:

> I am the supreme and fiery force who sets all living sparks alight and breathes forth no mortal things, but judges them as they are. Circling above the circumscribing circle with my superior wings, which is to say circling with wisdom, I have ordered the cosmos rightly. But I am also the fiery life of divine essence: I blaze above the beauty of the fields, I shine in the waters, I burn in the sun and the moon and the stars. And with the airy wind I quicken all things to life, as with an invisible life that sustains them all. For the air lives in *viriditas* and in the flowers, and the waters flow as if alive, and the sun lives within its own light, and when the moon has waned it is rekindled by the light of the sun and thereby lives anew, and the stars shine forth in their own light as though alive.[14]

Thus, *viriditas*, is the nonviolent power of our religious traditions and their practices (at their best); and it is the power of gardening. Planting is praying, and every prayer contains hope. Every prayer is a conversation—even if the labor, from time to time, seems one-sided.

But prayer with and through the Earth has a way of turning solipsism into relationship. Pray (plant) and you will receive an answer—a presence. Hope fulfilled.

JUSTICE AND ABUNDANCE

It is rare that my garden produces all that I hope for. There is a relentless logic of cause and effect—call it justice—that routinely thwarts my efforts to steer the course of *viriditas*. That logic is evident not only in the short Wisconsin growing season, and in my aversion to weeding, but also in all manner of pests and predators and plagues.

For instance, each of the past six years, our tomatoes have wilted from what I have learned to recognize as "late blight." It is caused, I guess, by a fungus. My garden is adjacent to an old-growth forest, and those woods generate all sorts of lichens, mosses, and fungi, including an occasional morel, which we appreciate! But those woods also probably produce the fungus that causes late blight in tomatoes. And once the spores are in the soil, the only treatments involve replacing the soil as deep as four inches deep or treating the plants with a fungicide.

I'm committed to organic gardening: no toxic chemicals in my veggies. But I do spray with sulfur—an organic compound that at least slows the attack of the fungi, which work their way up from the roots through the central stem, gradually wilting leaves, then entire peripheral stems, and eventually the entire plant. I'd guess that late blight has reduced the yield of my tomatoes by at least fifty percent over the past years. I don't spray often enough, or catch the signs early enough, to keep it from spreading.

Still, that logic of justice doesn't stop us from eating some nice juicy tomatoes straight from the vine all summer and well into October. Usually, we even have enough to freeze or can if we're so inclined. I like using our fresh-frozen tomatoes in the chili that I regularly make in winter to accompany Green Bay Packer football games.

And the garden (bad as I am at tending it) always manages to surprise me with its bounty: green beans by the bagful; jalapenos so plentiful I can make salsa; eggplant enough to make baba ghanoush. So, while I lament that justice of cause and effect in the garden, there's also a flowering of abundance—rampant, redolent, and juicy. Recognizing that abundance and fostering it, even if not perfect, may be a key to deep peace for our planet, and for us. To be driven by scarcity (and fear) generates the kind of us/them dualisms at the root of conflict. To be engaged by a surprising abundance generates gratitude and relationship (even a feast!)

As Regina Schwartz has put it in *The Curse of Cain*, monotheistic believers have often been driven by a logic of scarcity: there's only one God, only so much grace to go around, only one way to the promised land.[15] And yet, why do we make this assumption that one God (ours) is the only manifestation of the Sacred? What arrogance! Even more, even if there is only one God, given what our traditions (plural) generally teach us about God-ness, isn't it likely that there's enough to go around?

In other words, shifting from an implicit logic of scarcity (and survival)—at the root of capitalism—to one of abundance and flourishing—at the root of every garden—is to put into practice what I call the capacity of our religious traditions to generate "engaged empathy." That is, people of faith generally don't shy away from recognizing suffering: we treat the wilting tomato when we see it. But we also recognize that means matter. *How* we engage is as important as that we do so. We engage (again, at our best) with empathy, trying to sustain the flourishing for as many as we can, while recognizing that finally life is suffering, as the Buddha taught. Kimmerer puts it like this: "All of our flourishing is mutual." And like this: "A garden is a nursery for nurturing connection, the soil for cultivation of practical reverence." And this: "Appreciation begets abundance."[16] Gardening can help shift our sense of the world from scarcity and fear to a world filled with abundance, and offer visions for a verdant earth in ages to come.

As I write this in mid-April, my garden lies fallow after winter, but as the snow melts (we had a light dusting this morning) it is softening and opening and will soon be ready. As the Apostle Paul put it in Romans 8, the "creation waits with eager longing" for us to join with it in generating abundant life.

BEYOND PURITY

Mary Douglas tried to teach us decades ago that trying to impose purity on the inherent messiness of life is impossible. Yet still we try, and fail. Getting dirty is inevitable in gardening. I invariably drag clumps of earth into our house after a day of tilling or watering. That experience of impurity—of dirt out of place—can remind us of our own fragility and prepare us to endure with equanimity the inexorability of suffering and death. I learned this lesson again very recently.

On the last day of April, as this essay sat untouched at this very point, my mother, Barbara Joy Olsen Pahl, died. My brother, who is an M.D.; my son, Nathan; and I found her lying on the floor of her bathroom after we hadn't heard from her for a couple of days. "A massive heart-attack," said the coroner. "She died before she hit the ground," said my brother.

It wasn't unusual for her to go radio silent for a few days. Since my dad died last January, she'd cultivated a very strong network of female friends and neighbors. She was enjoying her independence and leading an active life. On the Friday before she died, we'd attended my grandson's basketball game and then went out for pizza with the extended family at the spot I haunted in high school, though I hadn't visited for decades. Neither had my mom. The pizza tasted exactly like she and I remembered it, we agreed.

Then, on the Sunday she died, she went to church (as usual), hosted my son and grandsons for brunch, went to a concert in the afternoon, and that evening called me on the phone. We talked for a half-hour. Then, she talked to my daughter Rheanne for forty-five minutes. The last words she heard from me were, "I love you." The last words she spoke to our daughter, to anyone, were spoken to Rheanne: "You're practically perfect, and I love you."

My tears as I write those words point to the absence that is as recognizable an experience as any notion of presence, when we are honest. There is more unknown than we can ever know. The past slips into memory. Parents die. And yet the garden awaits our labor.

Gardening is, or ought to be, a lesson in impermanence. The fragility of any plant is like our own fragility. "We are dust, and to dust we shall return," I intoned as we placed the urns holding my mother and father's ashes into the family plot. Purity, stability, control. . .it is all an illusion.

Douglas puts it like this:

> Whenever a strict pattern of purity is imposed on our lives it is either highly uncomfortable or it leads into contradiction if closely followed; and if not observed, hypocrisy. That which is negated is not thereby removed. The rest of life, which does not tidily fit the accepted categories, is still there and demands attention. The body, as we have tried to show, provides a basic scheme for all symbolism. There is hardly any pollution which does not have some primary physiological reference. As life is in the body it cannot be rejected outright.[17]

It is a peculiar penchant of Christians, shared by nationalists, and no doubt by other people, to devise systems that compress and displace dirt, taboo, the body, and sex into purity projects to transcend death.

I'm not having it. I like the dirt. I've always been drawn to taboo. My body, while ailing like those of others my age, is still my vehicle to experiences of friendship, laughter, music, joy, wonder, even ecstasy. Gardening grounds me in transience. In the garden I use my body to dig, rake, till, kneel, and sometimes even lay in the dirt. I breathe it in and smell it. I plant and water and pull and push and grunt and sweat. And then I do it again. And again. And again.

It was my maternal grandparents, Ruth and John Olsen, avid gardeners both, as well as dairy farmers, who first taught me this lesson. I was invited to be the emcee for their fiftieth wedding anniversary, in 1985. They were in their early eighties. I'd never heard their story, so I sat down to interview them in my parents' bedroom. I asked them questions about how they met, their first date, and then for a story about each of their five children (my mom was their oldest). My last question to them was, "What was the secret of your success, fifty years of marriage?"

Grandma Ruth spoke first, and said, "I'd say it was love, honor, and . . ." she paused, "determination." I told her I liked her answer.

Then Grandpa John spoke. "Somebody once said," he started, "if two people agree perfectly on everything, one of them is unnecessary." I laughed, and then he got a gleam in his blue eyes. "And," he went on, "it doesn't hurt to have a good love life."

Now, recall the scene. I'm sitting in my parents' bedroom talking with my grandparents about their love life. What do you say? So, I blurted out, "Oh, you had a good love life, did you?"

And they answered, in unison: "What do you mean, HAD?"

They gardened together liked they made love together. Maybe the love-making and the gardening were the same thing, in the end. Grounded in transience, we can be open to experience the embodied pleasures the world offers.

A BELOVED COMMUNITY OF KIN

We all live with a beloved community of kin—those present now, those present in memory, and those present to us in the planet and in the places of our lives. Any garden, obviously, is one of those (sacred) places, rich with kin. Any garden is redolent with our plant kin, in the present; our departed ancestors, in memory; and those with whom we connect through the community of gardeners and other forms of praying. And that extended community of beloved kin is a solace for suffering, a source of deep peace, a way to flourish with and through fragility and loss.

This is a new recognition for me, into which I continue to grow.

In 2014, I was invited to attend a conference at Cambridge University that brought together scholars of the humanities, like me, with scholars of evolutionary biology. It was an exciting mash-up. My greatest takeaway was that Darwin was wrong about natural selection. It's not the survival of the fittest, one biologist summarized, "it's the survival of the most cooperative."[18]

Recently, I've been researching kinship, as I prepare to write a book on "Siblinghood." What I'm discovering is that Darwin was really, really wrong. Ecuadorian environmental writer and activist Lisa María Madera puts it like this:

> The traits that propel natural selection include survival of the creative, survival of the cooperative, survival of the welcoming, survival of the bridge builders, survival of the observant, survival of the seductive, survival of the inclusive, survival of the artistic, survival of the resilient, survival of the strategic, survival of the flexible, survival of the colorful, survival of the transparent, survival of the musical, survival of the fragrant, survival of the generous, survival of the impervious, survival of the ingenious, survival of the bold, survival of the shy.[19]

The point should be clear. Survival isn't only, or even primarily, a matter of competition.

Novelist Richard Powers, author of *The Overstory*, a wonderful book about the kinship of trees, expands the point:

> Our capacity to will ourselves into kinship with seemingly remote creatures is in fact an exaptation: something that natural processes could never have selected for but that now ...presents altogether new opportunities for thriving. It seems to me that this ability to see our future contained in the fortune of others, a kinship based not on relatedness but on common cause, may be the one feature of self-awareness capable of saving our species from all the other potent (and potentially fatal) adaptations that evolution has endowed us with.

> [In] the messy domain of human social relations, ["fitness"] gives way to the idea of nurture kinship, in which community tends to be strengthened and sustained when the perceived kinship between

nurturer and nurtured yields more to the community than it costs the nurturer to give. Blood ties give way to proxy relations and fictive kinship—kinship grounded in shared place, shared practices, and shared narratives, both measurable and imaginary.[20]

A new way of thriving opens when we imagine our kin not only in our blood relations, but in the shared yield of all our relations that generates gifts to the community: something, in terms my Lutheran kin would recognize, like grace.

My mom used to stand with me on the edge of my garden, admiring my potatoes. "The ancestors are smiling down at you," she'd say. "Hilda and Oscar and Ruthie and John would be so proud of you," she'd say. This was, of course, her indirect Norwegian way of saying that she was proud of me.

Such a projection and displacement might lead to others, no less imagined, no less richly fictive, and yet no less potent and true. "A garden is the way that the land," Kimmerer puts it, "says, 'I love you.'"[21]

Can we believe that? Come taste our pesto—and tell me what you think.

NOTES

1. I developed the category of "deep peace" to differentiate religious activity that fosters the capacity to flourish (which is all I mean by "peace") from so-called "negative" peace, the absence of war—which I call "basic peace," and from "policy peace," those capacities to flourish that flow from political engagement. See Pahl, *Fethullah Gülen*.
2. This four-fold way to characterize "religion" in terms of discourses, practices, communities, and institutions comes from Lincoln, *Holy Terrors*.
3. Csikszentmihalyi, Flow.
4. Kimmerer, *Braiding Sweetgrass*, 69.
5. Kimmerer, *Braiding Sweetgrass*, 69.
6. Arendt, *On Violence*, 44.
7. King, "Where Do We Go From Here?"
8. Kimmerer, *Braiding Sweetgrass*, 123.
9. Pahl, *Empire of Sacrifice*.
10. See, for instance, Sacks, *The Dignity of Difference*; Leymah Gbowee, *Mighty Be Our Powers*; and Pahl, *Fethullah Gülen*.
11. I explore *viriditas* in some detail in Chapter 10 of *Shopping Malls and Other Sacred Spaces*. The quotes come from Fox (ed.), *Illuminations of Hildegard of Bingen*, 30–31.
12. Ross, "Hildegard of Bingen Composes the Cosmos."
13. Ross, "Hildegard of Bingen Composes the Cosmos."
14. Ross, "Hildegard of Bingen Composes the Cosmos."

15. Schwartz, *The Curse of Cain*.
16. Kimmerer, *Braiding Sweetgrass*, 166, 126, 116.
17. Douglas, *Purity and Danger*, 202.
18. Some of the papers, including mine, co-authored with James K. Wellman, are collected in Antonello and Gifford (eds.), *Can We Survive Our Origins?*
19. Madera, "The Wondrous W'aka World," 25.
20. Powers, "A Little More Than Kin," 75. *The Overstory* won Powers the Pulitzer Prize in 2019.
21. Kimmerer, *Braiding Sweetgrass*, 123.

REFERENCES

Antonello, Pierpalo, and Paul Gifford, eds. *Can We Survive Our Origins? Readings in René Girard's Theory of Violence and the Sacred*. Studies of Violence, Mimesis and Culture. East Lansing: Michigan State University Press, 2015.

Arendt, Hannah, *On Violence*. New York: Harcourt,1969.

Bingen, Hildegard. *The Illuminations of Hildegard of Bingen*. Edited by Matthew Fox. Rochester, VT: Bear and Company, 2003.

Csikszentmihalyi, Mihaly. *Flow: The Psychology of Optimal Experience*. New York: Harper Perennial, 2008.

Douglas, Mary. *Purity and Danger: An Analysis of the Concepts of Pollution and Taboo*. Chicago: University of Chicago Press, 1966.

Gbowee, Leymah. *Mighty Be Our Powers: How Prayer, Sisterhood and Sex Changed a Nation at War*. New York: Beast Books, 2013.

Kimmerer, Robin Wall. *Braiding Sweetgrass: Indigenous Wisdom, Scientific Knowledge, and the Teachings of Plants*. Minneapolis: Milkweed, 2013.

King, Martin Luther, Jr. "Where Do We Go From Here?" Annual report delivered at the 11th Convention of the Southern Christian Leadership Conference, Atlanta, GA, August 16, 1967. http://www-personal.umich.edu/~gmarkus/MLK_WhereDoWeGo.pdf

Lincoln, Bruce. *Holy Terrors: Thinking about Religion after 9/11*. Chicago: University of Chicago Press, 2006.

Madera, Lisa María. "The Wondrous W'aka World: Lessons from Pach Mama in the Face of Despair." In *Kinship: Belonging in a World of Relations* Vol. 2: Place, edited by Gavin Van Horn, Robin Wall Kimmerer, and John Hausdoerffer. Libertyville, IL: Center for Humans and Nature, 2021.

Pahl, Jon. *Fethullah Gülen: A Life of Hizmet—Why a Muslim Scholar in Pennsylvania Matters to the World*. Clifton, NJ: Blue Dome, 2019.

———. *Empire of Sacrifice: The Religious Origins of American Violence*. New York: New York University Press, 2012.

———. *Shopping Malls and Other Sacred Spaces: Putting God in Place*. Grand Rapids, MI: Brazos, 2003.

Powers, Richard. "A Little More Than Kin." In *Kinship: Belonging in a World of Relations* Vol. 3: Partners, edited by Gavin Van Horn, Robin Wall Kimmerer, and John Hausdoerffer. Libertyville, IL: Center for Humans and Nature, 2021.

Ross, Alex. "Hildegard of Bingen Composes the Cosmos." *New Yorker*, February 6, 2023, https://www.newyorker.com/magazine/2023/02/06/hildegard-of-bingen-composes-the-cosmos.

Sacks, Jonathan. *The Dignity of Difference: How to Avoid the Clash of Civilizations*. New York: Bloomsbury Continuum, 2002.

Schwartz, Regina, *The Curse of Cain: The Violent Legacy of Monotheism*. Chicago: University of Chicago Press, 1997.

JOHAN ROELAND

THE SLOW GARDEN: GARDENING AS DECELERATION[1]

"A SANCTUARY FROM THE FRENZY AND TUMULT OF HISTORY"

In his book-length essay *Gardens: An Essay on the Human Condition*, the Stanford-based scholar Robert Pogue Harrison argues that in Western culture "it has been the garden, whether real or imaginary, that has provided sanctuary from the frenzy and tumult of history."[2] Gardens are "a kind of haven, if not a kind of heaven," a "counterforce to history's deleterious drives."[3] Harrison continues: "Where history unleashes its destructive and annihilating forces, we must, if we are to preserve our sanity, to say nothing of our humanity, work against and in spite of them. We must seek out healing or redemptive forces and allow them to grow in us."[4]

Harrison supports this basic idea by referring to famous gardens from mythology, philosophy, and literature. He also refers to well-known gardens such as the Jardin du Luxembourg in Paris and the gardens around the Villa Borghese in Rome. This present article is based on observations of lesser-known, even everyday gardens that generally do not make it into garden magazines and books about gardens. It is based on conversations with passionate gardeners who will not be included in the history books with Plato, Epicurus, or Voltaire[5]—well-known philosophers who all shared a fascination for the garden. But Harrison's basic notion that the garden is a safe haven is also heard in the conversations I had with these gardeners. They, too, seek a safe place in the garden. For them it is a place free from "the frenzy and tumult of history"—where history today has a very specific frenzy in store, namely the frenzy of raging time and the lack of time, a frenzy accompanied by experiences of busyness, stress, and haste. For these gardeners, the garden offers peace and rest, and gardening is experienced as a form of "deceleration": a dimension of gardening that I will explore in more detail in this contribution.

While most people think of gardens in terms of space, this essay approaches gardens through the phenomenon of time. I will discuss the background against which this approach to the garden becomes meaningful, namely the contemporary "culture of speed"[6] that is so decisive for the human condition in late modern society. To properly understand this culture of speed and the way in which the garden relates to it, the first step is to analyze the concept of time.

ON TIME AND THE EXPERIENCE OF TIME

We tend to think of time as a universal, general category: something that exists outside of us, that is always the same everywhere, something that is simply there, as a natural thing. Time is often understood as a quantitative fact: it can be divided into units such as seconds, hours, days, months, and years. Time is often equated with (and limited to) clock time. Yet this intuitive definition of time turns out to be problematic, and of a recent date: our perception of time as a universal, "timeless," abstract, and quantifiable category is not very old. Many people have lived under time regimes in which time is organized, structured, and configured differently.

Time as clock time appears strongly to be related to the industrial way of life that emerged in the nineteenth century, the age of clock time, which would develop into the dominant (and self-evident) form of time in the centuries to come. The capitalism-industrialization complex was decisive in this.[7] The pursuit of the highest possible circulation speed of capital (capitalism) and the highest possible production (industrialization) required a manageable, quantifiable, and manipulable form of time. Not only did clock time become the dominant form of time in factories; clock time also became decisive in everyday life, which entailed a break with the "natural" time (in which the day and night rhythm and the seasons played a greater role) that had been dominant for centuries.

But the nineteenth century was also significant for the perception of time in another way. The nineteenth century was—and I follow the cultural sociologist Tomlinson here—the century of the *acceleration* of time. And here too the capitalism-industrialization complex turned out to be crucial. After all, in industrial-capitalist logic, the adage "time is money" applies. In other words, it is lucrative to achieve more in less time. It is this logic that has continued to have a major impact on processes of mechanization and automation (developing fast, labor-saving machines, devices, vehicles, digital assets, etc.), on the standardization and automation of processes, and on the emergence of scientific disciplines and applied sciences in which the key word is efficiency and in which "the modern principles of control, planning, organization and regulation"[8] are central.[9] This specific science and technology-based acceleration of time started in the nineteenth century and took off in the twentieth and twenty-first centuries, when a culture of speed would become dominant not only in industry and business, but also beyond. Everything must be done quickly, faster, preferably immediately: food, information technology, delivery of goods and services, knowledge, cultural products, reading, transport, travelling, shopping, and so on and so forth. Moreover, as Tomlinson argues, in a culture of speed, speed is a positive thing that is associated with vitality, dynamism, and progress.[10]

In terms of speed, mobility, productivity, comfort (in the case of so-called "domestic technologies" such as washing machines, freezers and refrigerators, and digital equipment), and ease of use, this acceleration has a lot to offer—at least for certain sectors, groups, and people. However, there is also a downside, or rather a whole host of downsides, including the growing contradiction between those who benefit from acceleration and those who suffer from it; the huge impact this acceleration has on the climate (in terms of waste, exploitation of resources and people, and CO_2 emissions); its negative impact on people who are confronted with time-related problems such as time pressure, haste, stress, the feeling of being constantly short of time, the pressure to keep up, and burnout complaints; being "out of sync" with natural and biological processes on the one hand and social, cultural, and economic processes dominated by clock time on the other;[11] and finally, as Hartmut Rosa argues in his well-known *Resonance*, a lack of resonance or deep connection with the world, other people, and ourselves, due to the fastness and hence superficiality of these connections.[12]

Because the downsides of acceleration weigh heavily, attempts are made to experience time in a different way, to break through the dominance of clock time, to "decelerate," to slow down. This results in numerous movements, activities, products, and programs that use the designation of "slow": slow food, Citta Slow,[13] slow academia,[14] slow cinema, slow sex, slow fashion, slow medicine, slow parenting, slow education, and slow travel, to name a few. Other activities such as meditation, yoga and mindfulness are not always directly referred to as "slow," but deceleration is certainly part of it. In all cases, we are dealing with attempts to escape the constant acceleration of contemporary life and to regain quality of life instead—a quality that is understood in terms of slowing down.

TIME AND THE GARDEN

Deceleration is also one of the recurring themes in my conversations with passionate gardeners. For many of them, the garden is a place of slowing down, a place where they escape from the speed of everyday life, a place where they—to use a few (somewhat cliché) expressions I often hear among gardeners—"unwind" and experience "being in the here and now." The garden is a refuge for them, a place to withdraw from everyday life that is perceived as "busy." Like many of us, these gardeners assume the garden creates a special kind of space, but they also understand gardens as a special kind of *time*.

The contrast between a busy life and the tranquility of the garden was expressed very strongly in an interview I conducted years ago with a middle-aged woman who lived in the center of Utrecht. She barely had a garden around her house, but she rented an allotment garden on the outskirts of the city. For her too, slowing down was one of the most cherished aspects of gardening, in which she not only described the contrast between a hectic (working) existence and the tranquility of gardening, but also the contrast between the city and her garden on the edge of town. In her view, the city stands for speed, vitality, movement, development, activity, dynamism, an association that many have with the city. The city is, as a metaphor by Carl Honoré suggests, a "giant particle accelerator."[15] That dynamic of city life made the city both attractive and burdensome to this woman. The garden offers a certain balance between the acceleration of the city and the deceleration that the garden stimulates. As mentioned, her garden was on the outskirts of the city, in a marginal place. This, of course, is simply the consequence of city development policies in a crowded and compact city. However, for this woman this marginality was significant. It meant her garden was hidden from the busy city life. It provided a separated, special space that, in turn, provided her with a separated, special sense of time.

It was after this interview that I started thinking about gardens in terms of "heterotopia." Michel Foucault used this concept to designate spaces and places that are different and escape the continuity of everyday space: work, living, moving, etc. These other spaces have their own dynamics, their own logic, their own way of doing things that differs from that of the ordinary, everyday space. These other spaces are of a different order and escape the existing social and cultural order—in this case the order of accelerated time. Sometimes these places are escapist, meant to escape the normalized order. Sometimes they are revolutionary, intended to overthrow the normal order. Sometimes—and I think that is the case for most of the gardeners my students and I have spoken to—these other places are meant to find balance in an accelerated world. In this sense, gardens function as "slow zones": areas in which a different regime of time operates than in everyday life, in which the possibility of "applying the brakes"[16] is practiced, in which the opportunity is offered for "periodic escape and retreat from a fast-paced life."[17] As such, the garden is not simply a heterotopos but a hetero*chronos* as well.

The garden has a potential to offer deceleration. This slowing down is discussed by gardeners in different terms. "Unwinding," "catching your breath," and "de-stressing" are descriptions that explicitly contrast with the restlessness and stress associated with the pressure and acceleration that are so characteristic of contemporary everyday life. Words such as "attention," "being in the here and now," and "mindfulness" also introduce this contrast and refer to several consequences of the current culture of speed. The notion of attention contrasts with the constant distraction associated with the lack of time and the lack of attentive, committed involvement with things. The notions of "being in the here and now" and "being mindful" (experiences that are also central to contemporary forms of spirituality and meditation) contrast with the feeling of losing oneself in the hectic pace of existence.

In short, the garden helps in deceleration. The garden can be a heterotopic place that gives rise to a *heterochronos*, where a different regime of time reigns, a regime that helps you to slow down. The garden offers a different experience of time, from which the gardener harvests the benefits of rest, attention, and awareness.

THE SLOW GARDEN

It should be clear that the garden does not *necessarily* decelerate. After all, the garden can be one of our many responsibilities that require attention and time, even if that time is not available. Some moments in the year can be experienced as compelling and busy: autumn forces us to clear away the dying leaves, and in spring the garden demands constant attention, if it is not to become overgrown. Deceleration is not automatically a given in the garden; it only exists by virtue of intentional action. In other words, it is a conscious choice to shut oneself off from the pace outside the garden when working in the garden.

At the same time, the garden is ideally suited as a "slow zone" for several reasons. First, there is the simple fact that the gardener has relative autonomy in the garden. Gardening as a hobby, as a leisure activity, is usually not subject to the time-related norms that play a role in our working existence, especially the norms of productivity, efficiency, and work-related forms of discipline and regulation.

Secondly, the garden itself uses a relatively slow rhythm, namely the rhythm of nature determined by the seasons, the "slow pace of natural time," as the British psychiatrist and gardener Sue Stuart-Smith put it.[18] For the gardener, herein lies a break with a modern conception of time, which attempts precisely to break the rhythm of nature, to separate time from the "temporariness of the body, nature and the cosmos"[19] and replace it with an alternate form of time (clock time) and speed it up. Compared to the accelerated time of modernity, connecting to the rhythm of nature quickly slows down.

Thirdly, the garden forces one to postpone—and in that sense offers a counterpoint to what Tomlinson sees as the next step in the culture of speed: the "culture of instantaneity," which is "a culture accustomed to rapid delivery, ubiquitous availability and the instant gratification of desires."[20] I do not mean to say that the garden does not give instant gratification; after all, gardeners perceive gardening itself as satisfying. But it is true that gardening is accompanied by delay. After all, growth and flowering cannot be forced into acceleration. It needs time, not only the time to grow, but also the time for the breakdown and fall needed to re-emerge in a new spring. The gardener has no control over nature's time and must submit to it.

If the time of the garden is respected by the gardener, the garden offers a place of rest, attention, awareness, and balance—and as such a refuge in which the gardener withdraws, even for a moment, from the constant impact of accelerated time on our daily lives.

NOTES

1. A previous version of this article was published in Dutch in the Dutch-Belgian journal *Streven* (October 2020).
2. Harrison, *Gardens*, ix.
3. Harrison, *Gardens*, x.
4. Harrison, *Gardens*, x.
5. I started my research on gardening in 2013, during a period I spent at home due to burnout. At that time, I was unable to do much, and I hoped that gardening could help me in my recovery process. However, because I did not have any experience with gardening, I had to ask a gardener from my village for advice. During my conversations with her, I suddenly realized that the language that

she used was familiar to me: there were many expressions that I recognized from my research into contemporary lived religion and spirituality. I started my research on the interconnections between spirituality and gardening not long after I went back to work. I did my first in-depth interview in 2013, and I visited gardens, gardeners, and garden architects. Students in my course on lived religion and popular culture were asked to conduct an in-depth interview with a passionate gardener as well; in 2014 and 2015, my students did 26 interviews. I added two more interviews to my dataset in 2018. In this article, I make use of these interviews and conversations; quotes are taken from these interviews.

6. Tomlinson, *The Culture of Speed*.
7. Adam, *Time*, 73.
8. Tomlinson, *The Culture of Speed*, 19.
9. Adam, *Time*, 116.
10. Tomlinson, *The Culture of Speed*, 4.
11. Martineau, *Time, Capitalism and Alienation*, 2.
12. Rosa, *Resonance*.
13. Honoré, *In Praise of Slow*, 76.
14. Berg and Seeber, *The Slow Professor*, xviii.
15. Honoré, *In Praise of Slow*, 81.
16. Tomlinson, *The Culture of Speed*, 157.
17. Connolly, *Neuropolitics*, 144, quoted by Tomlinson, *The Culture of Speed*, 158.
18. Stuart-Smith, *The Well-Gardened Mind*, 20.
19. Adam, *Time*, 115.
20. Tomlinson, *The Culture of Speed*, 74.

REFERENCES

Adam, Barbara. *Time*. Cambridge: Polity Press, 2004

Berg, Maggie, and Barbara K. Seeber. *The Slow Professor: Challenging the Culture of Speed in the Academy*. Toronto: University of Toronto Press, 2016.

Connolly, William E. *Neuropolitics: Thinking, Culture, Speed*. Minneapolis: University of Minnesota Press, 2002.

Harrison, Robert P. *Gardens: An Essay on the Human Condition*. Chicago: University of Chicago Press, 2008.

Honoré, Carl. *In Praise of Slow: How a Worldwide Movement Is Challenging the Cult of Speed*. New York: Harper Collins, 2004.

Martineau, Jonathan. *Time, Capitalism and Alienation: A Socio-Historical Inquiry into the Making of Modern Time*. Leiden: Brill, 2015.

Rosa, Hartmut. *Resonance: A Sociology of Our Relationship to the World*. Cambridge: Polity, 2019.

Stuart-Smith, Sue. *The Well-Gardened Mind: The Restorative Power of Nature*. New York: Scripter, 2020.

Tomlinson, John. *The Culture of Speed: The Coming of Immediacy*. Los Angeles: SAGE, 2007.

ROW LIGHT

CHILDREN OF SPACE[1]

Here I am, autumn again
unable to go inside my own house
my wings too broad, even folded.
But Prophet writes,
unbend the head,
release the breath,
don't bear structures not meant for you.

Child of space,
you, "restless in rest," foot tap
into afternoon lulls, feel shame melt
pleasantly down the inner arm,
kissing a streak of salt on the skin.

Waiting for the floors to crack up
finally feels within reason;
expecting every dam to burst
no longer diagnosable,
but rather, wildly sensible.

Live with the dormant knowledge
that we are not active agents
in the universal body;
that, though we may displace all order,
we cannot rage on command.

I don't yet know what will happen
when eyes shut tightly with the gate.

Enough nights in, the room might leak
some new and terrifying ease —
in such a case, I'd quickly pile the furniture
to save what's still unhomed in me.

Would I lay down my life for comfort?
Ever awake, at work in this mind,
I'd drain the passion from these cheeks
till I'm that dead, unopened thing,
while others trace my walls
with their lily pad soft palms.

The Prophet compares material gain to lust;
so when you feel over-full,
begin to host body spasms,
or tchotchkes line up at your baseboards
in newly unified battalions,
we'll have to have our own revolution —

freedom deserves a still blank wall
for everything we haven't thought of.

> *You shall not fold your wings that you may pass through doors, nor bend your head that they strike not against a ceiling, nor fear to breathe lest walls should crack and fall down. You shall not dwell in tombs made by the dead for the living… But you, children of space, you restless in rest, you shall not be trapped nor tamed.*
> —Kahlil Gibran[2]

NOTES
row-light.com
1. "Children of space" is defined by Kahlil Gibran's editor Suheil B. Bushrui as "those freed from the shackles of materialism."
2. Kahlil Gibran, *The Prophet: A New Annotated Edition* (New York: Simon and Schuster, 2012), 33.

REVIEW BY IRINA SHEYNFELD

EBONY G. PATTERSON AT THE NEW YORK BOTANICAL GARDEN:
Enter Vultures

> "Southern trees bear strange fruit
> Blood on the leaves and blood at the root."
> —"Strange Fruit"[1]

In the fall of 2023, something exciting took place at the New York Botanical Garden. Multidisciplinary artist Ebony G. Patterson (b.1981) released a wake of vultures inside the Conservatory and upon the Enid A. Haupt Conservatory lawn. For those who do not know, a group of large raptors circling the dead is sometimes referred to as a "wake." Patterson's show, entitled *...things come to thrive...in the shedding...in the molting...*, and which uses sculpture and plant life to evoke a dark past, was on view until October 22, 2023. The artist wished to let her work fall apart and die a natural death at the end of its run in the fall.

When I visited the garden in the middle of October, the plants were flourishing in a decadent final burst of color and fury, but in the shadows, the rot was already spreading its first bloom. Patterson's latest show explores life cycles of decay, regrowth, and regeneration, and her highly immersive work thrusts her audience into a story that she weaves from live plants, glass-cast body parts, and foam-cast black vultures.

Patterson is a young artist from Jamaica whose work is highly narrative and site-specific. *...things come to thrive...* is immersive and thought-provoking—with her work at the Botanical Garden, she intended to ruffle some feathers. In an interview with Thelma Golden, the director and chief curator of the Studio Museum in Harlem, Patterson said that she had wondered who the people who came to the New York Botanical Garden were. The artist went on to claim that they were older retired white women,

> ...and I just kept thinking about these women who would come because of the peonies, or they would come because of the roses. And

I thought, "What would it mean to make the person who would come because of the peonies just a little annoyed, just a little bit?" Because I think that there's a fundamental importance in understanding what places like this come out of historically.[2]

The artist wanted to make viewers uncomfortable by highlighting the fact that many of the garden plants that they had come to admire originally

Figure 1. Irina Sheynfeld, *Ebony G. Patterson among her birds*, 2023, watercolor, ink, and mixed media collage.

arrived on the same boats as enslaved men and women. The show's cast-glass plants were modeled after extinct plants that did not survive relocation or perished like so many other beings who have been victims civilization's expansion. Patterson uses the aesthetic beauty of her work as bait; she entices her audience into a tangled maze of bloodred and lime green flowering hedges. There, the hunters are made to feel just a little bit hunted, though the metaphors are sometimes stretched a bit too thin.

Figure 2. Detail of *...things come to thrive...in the shedding...in the molting...*(2023) on Conservatory Lawn at The New York Botanical Garden. (Photo by Irina Sheynfeld)

Figures 3 and 4. Detail of ...*things come to thrive...in the shedding...in the molting...*(2023) on Conservatory Lawn at The New York Botanical Garden. (Photo by Irina Sheynfeld)

As visitors enter the Conservatory Lawn, they encounter a path that Patterson invites them to follow. It is here that visitors first see her black vultures, which have no bases, allowing the large birds to blend seamlessly into their surroundings—there are no barriers that separate their world from ours. Vultures invade the garden, and they beckon one to follow. Their sparkling black carbon bodies lure visitors deeper and deeper into the bushes. At first, birds appear to be roaming about idly, searching for food in the grass. They seem to be engaged with one another only casually, eyeing what morsels others have found. Their behavior appears to be ordinary and birdlike, but that soon changes. Patterson's engagement with the audience is akin to participatory shows like *Sleep No More*, where guests follow seemingly disjointed fragments of narrative by walking around the darkened McCormick Hotel and observing actors perform short bits in various rooms. As a result, each audience member comes away with their own version of the story. So it is here, that the perceived narrative is different for every viewer and changes, even when the same viewer walks through the maze.

It is not a coincidence that Patterson modeled her raptors after *Coragyps atratus*, otherwise known as the American Black Vulture. The artist uses some aspects of the raptors' voracious behavior to create a metaphor for the ravaging conquests of colonialism. Vultures grow up to twenty-six inches in length, with a wingspan of fifty-eight inches and an average weight of three to five pounds. They are not very large birds, but their aura of death and fear is outsized in our imagination. About twenty million vultures thrive worldwide—they are well adapted to living alongside people—and their ubiquity is perhaps one reason that people can't help but anthropomorphize these birds' actions. In *Vultures of the World*, Keith L. Bildstein describes vultures as gregarious, commensal, and highly social, though frequently aggressive.[3] Patterson appreciates the contradictory role that vultures play in the natural world. She also calls them the healers of the natural world. By devouring carrion, they play an essential part in the regenerative cycle of nature. In an interview with *Brooklyn Rail* editor Amanda Gluibizzi, Patterson points out that vultures' consumption of bodies is always an act of revealing what lies below the surface and that it can therefore be interpreted as an act of care that brings about regeneration and rebirth.[4]

As one moves deeper into the winding paths, the vultures' behavior shifts. Suddenly, it seems that they are no longer acting like birds. The raptors have become aware of themselves and each other. They appear to be at high attention, communicating in a highly organized manner about something very interesting that has been discovered deep inside the bushes. About ten of them appear in a lounging position, pointing their sharp beaks at something in the vegetation that, for the viewer, remains unknown and unseen. A few of them look back from the bushes. "Yes," they seem to say. "It is here."

The farther one penetrates the labyrinth, the more menacing and determined the birds appear to be. Some of their blue-black bodies blend into the purple vegetation, while others cut startling, dark silhouettes against lime-colored leaves. Formally, there is a push and pull between the light subjects and the dark background that reminds one of the classical rules of painting. And indeed, Patterson describes herself as more of a painter than a sculptor. The plants that surround the vultures create a rich, painterly backdrop, but they were not chosen solely based on their color. Many, such as the green and purple *Coleus*, the scarlet love-lies-bleeding, and the violet *Angelonia angustifolia* are transplants from Africa and Central America.

The foliage plays its own part in the world Patterson has created: it hides the vultures' actions and protects their secrets. It is a co-conspirator. It is also the most fragile part of the show, the part that will certainly die—most plants in the exhibit are annuals—and regenerate. The cycle of rebirth in Patterson's work suggests that what the vultures have consumed will not perish completely but rather change into something new and unexpected in the future. Patterson's birds sparkle and refract the light because of small pieces of broken glass, perhaps the same cut-glass that came from whatever it is they have devoured in the bushes. The glass seems to be now embedded into the vultures' ebony bodies, transforming them into something new and strange right before our eyes.

Inside the Conservatory, where *...things come to thrive...* continues, the secret is revealed. We discover body parts, mostly feet, that protrude from the same dense vegetation that proliferates on the lawns. Made from a translucent cast-glass they seem to be ghosts, shadows—negative spaces left by beings that are no more.

Finally, up above the exhibit, on a rough wooden scaffolding, sits a white peacock. It looks unfinished and, encased in a wooden frame, it is easy to miss. At first, it appears disjointed from to the rest of the show. One wonders, did installers forget to remove this piece before they opened the gates? Why is it here among the dwellers of this colorful netherworld? In the interview with Gluibizzi, Patterson explained

Figure 5. Detail of ...*things come to thrive...in the shedding...in the molting...* (2023) on Conservatory Lawn at The New York Botanical Garden. (Photo by Irina Sheynfeld)

that she had once observed a white peacock molting in a zoo. Its feathers were spread majestically, but it was molting. The peacock looked so unlike his usual splendid self that "...it almost seemed like the peacock was haunting its enclosure... it wasn't making any sounds...it was floating or hovering in this kind of ghostly way."[5]

Figure 6. Detail of ...*things come to thrive...in the shedding...in the molting...* (2023) on Conservatory Lawn at The New York Botanical Garden. (Photo by Irina Sheynfeld)

The nearly invisible, weak, and vulnerable peacock on a scaffolding is the key to Patterson's narrative. The majestic bird caught without its royal plumage captures the moment of weakness that is also a moment ripe for regeneration.

NOTES

1. Billie Holiday, vocalist, "Strange Fruit," lyrics by Lewis Allen, recorded 1939, Commodore.
2. *Ebony G. Patterson in Conversation with Thelma Golden.*
3. Bildstein, *Vultures of the World*, 22.
4. Patterson, "Ebony G. Patterson: …things come to thrive…in the shedding…in the molting…," interview by Gluibizzi with Tempestt.
5. Patterson, "Ebony G. Patterson: …things come to thrive…"

REFERENCES

Bildstein, Keith L. *Vultures of the World: Essential Ecology and Conservation.* Ithaca, NY: Comstock Publishing Associates, 2022.

Ebony G. Patterson in Conversation with Thelma Golden. New York Botanical Garden, 2023. https://www.youtube.com/watch?app=desktop&v=1a8YsQFDy0A.

Heinrich, Will. "Ebony G. Patterson Brings a Crowd to the New York Botanical Garden." *New York Times*, June 15, 2023. https://www.nytimes.com/2023/06/15/arts/design/patterson-new-york-botanical-garden-review-vultures.html.

Patterson, Ebony G. "Ebony G. Patterson: …things come to thrive…in the shedding…in the molting…" By Amanda Gluibizzi with Mimi Tempestt. *The Brooklyn Rail*. June 9, 2023. https://brooklynrail.org/events/2023/06/09/ebony-g-patterson-things-come-to-thrivein-the-sheddingin-the-molting.

REVIEW BY SAHIR DEWJI

Khoja-Moolji, Shenila. *Rebuilding Community: Displaced Women and the Making of a Shia Ismaili Muslim Sociality.* Oxford: Oxford University Press, 2023. 272 Pp. $29.95.

Shenila Khoja-Moolji's *Rebuilding Community: Displaced Women and the Making of a Shia Ismaili Muslim Sociality* is a fascinating look at place-making, focusing on Ismaili women's cultural memory and the ethics of communal care. The women whose stories the author narrates belong to the Shia Nizari Ismaili community, which recognizes and venerates a living Imam, known as Aga Khan IV. He is the forty-ninth hereditary Ismaili Imam who claims direct lineal descent from the first Shia Imam, Ali, and his successors. Today, this transnational community comprises culturally, linguistically, and ethnically diverse adherents and has settlements in over forty countries across the globe.

In particular, Khoja-Moolji's interlocutors form part of a specific subset of Ismailis of South Asian descent known as the Khoja, who make up a sizeable portion of the present Ismaili community. What connects these women is their love and affinity for the Imam—who "acts as a centripetal force that gives this community a distinct route to ethical action"—and their lived experience as "displaced people" who have performed and continue to partake in acts of care for their families and co-religionists. In retelling these women's narratives, Khoja-Moolji traces the (forced) migratory journeys of Ismaili Muslim women from colonial India to East Africa and then onto North America while detailing how Ismaili women forged community and reproduced bonds of spiritual kinship. As such, this work adds to the extant literature that examines settlement patterns of displaced Ismaili women in the diaspora and their lived experiences.

Drawing inspiration from scholarly works on feminist theories of ethics of care, Khoja-Moolji's monograph focuses on Ismaili women's agency. To illustrate the role of Ismaili women in critical moments, Khoja-Moolji looks at the voluntary acts of care that women undertake during times of displacement—due to forced migration—and in times of resettlement. In so doing, the author also disrupts the conventional theorization of ethics of care through an exploration of religion, which provides "additional morally compelling pathways to care and to the practice of collective social life." By theorizing an ethics of care that is tied closely to religion, Khoja-Moolji brilliantly illustrates how religious community is both the conduit of ethical action that facilitates women's acts of care as well as the product of the chosen acts undertaken by the women in this book.

The continual articulation of Ismaili sociality, as witnessed through the lives of the author's interlocuters, is deeply tied to interpretations and expressions of *seva*, or ethic of service. This salient trope appears throughout the lives of the multiple generations of women the author interviews. The long-standing practice of *seva* is given meaning by the performer, who is herself affected by circumstance, place, and positionality, and oriented by the principles of faith. Seva, therefore, is the mode through which an Ismaili ethico-religious subjectivity is produced. The author draws on oral histories, fieldwork, and memory texts to illuminate the ordinary acts of care undertaken by Ismaili women, which include a variety of activities that take place in the household and outside among non-kin (co-religionists).

Throughout her book, Khoja-Moolji treats *seva* performed by women as an "experience of Godly presence" that is animated through the interconnectivity of personal conviction and the Imam's guidance. She suggests that Ismaili sociality is mobilized by a strong religious kinship which itself is sustained by an ethico-religious collectivity that emanates from the Ismaili Imam but is also activated by personal action and a commitment to service (i.e., women's care activities). Such an understanding of Ismaili sociality, according to Khoja-Moolji, does not deny the shared ethnic and cultural ties of her interlocuters; rather, it brings into focus other motivations and conditions that cannot be explained by an ethno-cultural lens alone. These women's actions fall within the ambit of an ethico-religious worldview wherein everyday acts of care, kindness, generosity, and sacrifice are viewed more clearly through the lenses of spiritual kinship and ethical relationality.

One of the best aspects of the book is its attention to how the everyday acts of care generate notions and expressions of the sacred in place and in motion, the latter incorporating practices of diverse forms of devotional labor that are action oriented (e.g., bodies falling collectively in prostration, swaying in *dhikr*, preparing and sharing food, waking fellow co-religionists for prayers, driving a sick co-religionist to a clinic, as well as other similar movements) and help to foster and maintain spiritual ties among co-religionists. In striking detail, Khoja-Moolji pushes us to think critically about how we understand religious practice, morality and ethics, and the significance of migrant placemaking. She argues that the various activities performed by the women are best understood as devotional labor, wherein the different tasks are regarded "as blessings, privileges, and opportunities offered by the Imam." What makes Khoja-Moolji's study fascinating is how an overarching symbol, *seva*, engages women to undertake diverse forms of care work, thereby reinforcing "non-kin spiritual intimacy" and "form[ing] a tradition of placemaking that extends through time and space."

The book has seven chapters. The opening chapter describes the personal endeavor to undertake this study while also laying a clear theoretical framework for her approach to placemaking that builds on scholarly works from the fields of gender studies, religious studies, and urban studies. Khoja-Moolji, however, challenges current notions of placemaking by shifting attention to the spiritual and sensory dimensions. This shift allows her to take women's care work seriously as an important contribution to the Ismaili community's placemaking within the diaspora and poignantly argue how Ismaili women's placemaking activities give way to religious community formation. The chapter also includes an apt background of the Ismailis that pays attention to the socio-historical context that shaped the religious development of the community. The heart of the book is Chapters 2 through 6, in which Khoja-Moolji reconstructs the lifeworlds of Ismaili women migrants with the help of intimate interviews and meticulous archival work. Chapter 2 traces the displacement of Ismaili women from both East Africa and East Pakistan (i.e., present day Bangladesh). Through the memories and experiences of Khoja-Moolji's interlocutors, including her own mother, she captures how "Ismaili migrant women reinforced communal affinities while cultivating ethical sensibilities." Chapter 3 focuses on the efforts put forward by Ismaili women across three continents to reproduce sacred spaces by creating makeshift *jamatkhanas*, or community houses, when no fixed religious facility was set up, and even instilling an aura of sacrality in the most precarious of spaces such as steamboats and refugee camps.

In Chapter 4, the reader is transported to the realm of the sacred through Khoja-Moolji's retelling of miracle stories, or *moujza*, in Urdu. These narrative accounts of believers are shared amongst co-religionists with the purpose of reaffirming belief in Divine agency, via the Imam, which transcends both sacred and profane spaces. "*Moujza* stories are not usually found in formal Ismaili curricular texts; they are transmitted orally. Their telling is a form of cultural reproductive work aimed at cultivating religious sensibilities" in a similar manner to other caretaking practices performed by the author's interlocutors. In this sense, the story is the vehicle by which "the narrator not only cultivates a personal consciousness of God but also assists other practitioners in this endeavor." More importantly, *seva* is animated through the narration of the story itself—harnessing faith among the faithful listeners (an ethical act of community making)—but also within the stories themselves. These stories emerge in moments of strife or situations where community members find themselves in a position of helping their coreligionists—a form of *seva*. Chapter 5 is an analytical examination of cookbooks written by displaced women. Khoja-Moolji shows how the cookbook authors engage in a new form of emplacement through their texts, which play an important role in the reproduction of religious life in the diaspora. Food enables the authors and their readers to connect with the "home" of the past while also laying the foundation for home in new places. "The cookbook, then, is simultaneously mnemonic and aspirational. Like the *moujza* stories in the previous chapter, it is at once didactic (how to cook) and narrative (cookbooks often tell stories about their authors' journeys), acting to emplace the younger members within the community's historic and geographical experience through the habits of cooking and flavors of heritage foods." In this sense, the authors and their works participate in *seva* whereby the recipes and food help to solidify cultural tradition and reinforce the communal characteristics of Ismaili sociality.

The sixth chapter serves as a response to Chapter 2, centering the voices of second-generation displaced Ismaili women. Khoja-Moolji highlights similarities and differences in their approach to placemaking and sustaining an Ismaili sociality in comparison to that of the first generation. The comparative analysis in this chapter draws from interviews and a variety of literary, artistic, and scholarly materials. In keeping with the theme of *seva*, Khoja-Moolji explores the ways in which second-generation Ismaili women draw from earlier forms of service but also breathe new meaning(s) into the practice of *seva*. When it comes to the ways in which these women craft and engage with community, the reader can observe different forms and sites of Ismaili sociality wherein the centrality of *jamatkhana* and other Ismaili institutions has shifted but not diminished. This new generation simultaneously reckons with the communal past—including the role their forebears played in marginalizing indigenous Africans—while forging a new path for the future of the community. The concluding chapter provides an opportunity for the author to reflect on everyday actions of care that Ismaili women have practiced for generations and how their actions—defined by a universal and particular moral guidance—"have sustained the *jamat* against, and in the aftermath of, the dislocating effects of wars, forced migration, poverty, and racism."

Khoja-Moolji has written a marvelous book about lived Shia faith that centers on the pivotal role that women play in forging and sustaining an Ismaili sociality. *Rebuilding Community* is a well-researched and strongly theorized work within the limits of the author's goals. It seamlessly brings together many strands of contemporary theory from a number of fields including religious studies, affect studies, food studies, Islamic studies, diaspora studies, refugee studies, and gender studies. Building on ethnographic interviews, Khoja-Moolji's prose and storytelling prowess invite the reader to personally connect with the lives of the author's interlocutors. Drawing on extant literature across multiple disciplines, Khoja-Moolji's study drives home the significance of both the spiritual and reparative dimensions of women's care work, which "advance emplacement in the diaspora" and "harness belief (*iman*)." The book also successfully expands the narrow understanding of migrant placemaking beyond the rigid confines of space and place. Overall, Khoja-Moolji's monograph is a step toward codifying Ismaili women's memories and experiences into the official historical record of Ismailis that will serve as a repertoire of cultural memory for the Shia Nizari Ismaili community. In particular, any scholar interested in Shia or Ismaili studies will find this work enlightening for its analysis of women's care work practices through an ethico-religious perspective. Khoja-Moolji's thought-provoking work on women's placemaking is not limited to women's agency but involves other key components that include ethics, piety, and religio-moral codes. It is without doubt that the author's approach to Shia Ismaili women's placemaking puts forward a new understanding that will have lasting implications for scholars undertaking future research. *Rebuilding Community* will be of considerable value to academics across multiple fields as well as students and Ismailis who will be eager to read and reflect on shared stories of displacement and community building.

Mubarak, Hadia. *Rebellious Wives, Neglectful Husbands: Controversies in Modern Qur'anic Commentaries*. New York: Oxford University Press, 2022. 368 Pp. $32.99.

In this book, Hadia Mubarak seeks new answers to a question that has troubled feminist scholars of Islam for decades: "What is the origin of androcentrism or patriarchal readings in the genre of Qur'anic exegesis?" Mubarak authored earlier articles on feminist approaches to the Qur'an in the context of the classical and postclassical exegetes' interpretations of gender-related verses.[1] *Rebellious Wives, Neglectful Husbands* approaches this key question within the context of Q 2:228; 4:128; 4:34; and 4:3. It contributes to current scholarship in Islamic and gender studies by complicating dominant understandings of gender and interpretive authority within *tafsīr*, the field of Qur'anic interpretation.

In seven chapters, Mubarak highlights the genre's pluralist and polyvalent underpinnings. She focuses on the relationship between methods, meanings, and interpretive authority and asks how Muslim exegetes interpreted key Qur'anic verses on controversial gender issues: polygyny; marital rights and turbulence; the disciplining of rebellious wives; husbands' liability in case of neglect or disinterest; and men's privilege, or *daraja*, over women. Additional questions include how earlier readings of these verses were received and reinterpreted in modernity; how new methodological approaches shape hermeneutical findings; and how the way in which exegetes derive meaning alters our notions of tradition. In examining these questions, Mubarak successfully complicates the binary conception of the Qur'an as egalitarian and its commentaries as misogynistic texts.

Rebellious Wives, Neglectful Husbands's key intervention revolves around conceptions of interpretive authority. Some scholars, Mubarak notes, believe that feminist exegetes cannot gain interpretive authority within the tradition of *tafsīr* because exegetical authority "moves backwards" and can be achieved only by endorsing the same, often patriarchal, conclusions of previous interpreters.[2] Mubarak, on the other hand, argues that although authority is based on precedent, Qur'anic interpretations are repeated not necessarily because exegetes agree with previous ones, but because of the genre's genealogical nature. To claim authority within this genre, interpreters of the Qur'an must demonstrate mastery of the tradition by citing it, whether they agree with earlier readings or not. Mubarak demonstrates convincingly that a definitive interpretation of the Qur'an does not exist and that egalitarian readings can be derived without abandoning traditional exegetical methods.

To substantiate her arguments, Mubarak examines the "intersections of modernity and Sunni exegetical thought on women" and analyzes the works of four influential exegetes, Muhammad `Abduh (d. 1905), Rashid Rida (d. 1935), Sayyid Qutb (d. 1966), and Muhammad al-Tahir Ibn `Ashur (d. 1973). While comparing their interpretations with those of classical and postclassical Muslim scholars, she argues further that the theoretical significance of gender in modern Qur'anic exegesis reflects her interlocutors' attempt to push back against the colonial legacy of viewing Islam as unfit for modernity. Despite being caught inside of this dialectic, modern understandings of the Qur'an's position on gender are not only "a *response* to colonial, Western, or secular criticism of Islam but...also an attempt to clarify and elucidate the Qur'an's [true] meanings." Mubarak highlights the different ways in which these four scholars faced modernity's epistemological challenges. Muhammad `Abduh, for example, used this historical moment to emphasize the Qur'an's universal message and complicate the divide between a "Muslim" and a "non-Muslim" world.

Most illuminating is Mubarak's demonstration that exegetes have provided polyvalent answers to gender-related questions since before gender became one of modernity's discursive battlefields. She agrees with feminist scholars that "patriarchy is not inherent in the Qur'an but a product of certain male interpretations" and adds that, before modernity, the verses under discussion were sometimes "interpreted in ways that do not presume male authority as an inherent feature of the text." For example, the Abbasid historian and exegete Abu Ja`far al-Tabari (d. 923) views Q 2:228, according to which men have a "degree," or daraja, over their wives, as prescriptive. Rather than describing men's superior status, according to al-Tabari, this verse "prescribes a higher degree of ethical behavior for husbands." While his interpretation might not have been common, it was not "lost in the ashes of exegetical history," as Mubarak suggests. Indeed, late Ottoman thinkers like the Egyptian poet ʿAisha Taymur (d. 1902) argued along similar lines, a point that bolsters Mubarak's assessment that *tafsīr* is not monolithic and continues to evolve by preserving discordant views.[3]

Rebellious Wives, Neglectful Husbands is the most detailed study to be attempted so far within *tafsīr* studies as regards constructions of gender in modern Sunni Islam. The success of this work also lies in its systematic approach. Mubarak juxtaposes a multiplicity of exegetical views with detailed references to the changing religious, political, and social circumstances in which ʿAbduh, Rida, Qutb, and al-Tahir Ibn ʿAshur lived. Moreover, she is meticulous in illustrating methodological differences and how they inform interpretations. Although, from the 1940s onward, Qutb increasingly saw the world through a Manichaean and anti-Western lens, his literary training allowed him to ponder the interactions of sound and meaning and identify a musical rhythm for each Qur'anic chapter. Qutb's view of Islam as a "complete system" informed his reading of Q 4:34 which ascribes *qiwama*, often translated as "leadership," to men. The discursive logic Qutb adopts differs from that of premodern exegetes in two central ways. First, he frames men's "superior standing" as beneficial to women, since it supposedly protects them and the institution of marriage. Second, rather than describing marriage as a contractual relationship between two people, he views it "through the prism of the [nuclear] family as the basic social unity of society."

Mubarak compellingly comments on the ways in which the exegetical tradition conveys authority to modern exegetes without, however, forcing them to reach the same conclusions as the classical and postclassical interpreters. While drawing attention to the tradition's polyvalent views on gender-related verses, Mubarak suggests that, before dismissing this tradition a priori, scholars of Islam ought to consider its methods, which have offered Muslim communities the ability to derive meaning and negotiate historical change, with greater care. Surprisingly, while ʿAbduh, Rida, and Qutb geared their works toward audiences beyond the scholarly class, they also "introduced a higher level of subjectivity to their commentaries." On the other side, al-Tahir Ibn ʿAshur's philological exegesis and his focus on methodological continuity with previous exegetical works led to new outcomes that explicitly challenged the rigidity of Salafi and other paradigms.

This book moves *tafsīr* studies away from constructions of (pre) modern Islam as inherently misogynistic and monolithic. However, Mubarak's decision to leave aside female authors who have not produced commentaries upon the entire Qur'an but have published, at least since the late nineteenth century, articles about the Qur'anic verses discussed here has serious consequences. The result of this exclusion is that women's discussions on male authority that have occurred beyond the Euro-American academy are largely absent. Ironically, her readers might get the impression that Muslim women assumed a secondary role within modern Qur'anic exegesis. Despite this limit, Mubarak's conclusion about the inner logics of interpretive authority offers hope, as she writes, to future scholars of this "nascent field" to "have a broader selection of commentaries to explore."

NOTES

1. See Mubarak, "Breaking the Interpretive Monopoly" and Mubarak, "Change Through Continuity."
2. Hidayatullah, *Feminist Edges of the Qur'an*, 179–80.
4. Zaman, Review of *Tolerance and Coercion in Islam*, 471. On this key point Mubarak references Asad, *The Idea of an Anthropology of Islam*, 14; MacIntyre, *Whose Justice? Which Rationality?*, 22; and Zaman, *The Ulama in Contemporary Islam*, 4.

REFERENCES

Asad, Talal. *The Idea of an Anthropology of Islam*. Washington, DC: Center for Contemporary Ara Studies/Georgetown University, 1986.

Hidayatullah, Aysha. *Feminist Edges of the Qur'an*. Oxford: Oxford University Press, 2014.

MacIntyre, Alasdair. *Whose Justice? Which Rationality?*. Notre Dame, IN: University of Notre Dame Press, 1984.

Mubarak, Hadia. "Breaking the Interpretive Monopoly: A Re-Examination of Verse 4:34." *Hawwa* 2, no. 3 (2004): 261–89.

———. "Change Through Continuity: A Case Study of Q. 4:34 in Ibn ʿĀshūr's al-Tahrīr wa'l-tanwīr." *Journal of Qur'anic Studies* 20, no. 1 (2018): 1–27.

Zaman, Muhammad Qasim. *The Ulama in Contemporary Islam: Custodians of Change*. Princeton, NJ: Princeton University Press, 2002.

———. Review of *Tolerance and Coercion in Islam: Interfaith Relations in the Muslim Tradition*, by Yohanan Friedmann. *The Journal of Religion* 87, no. 3 (2007): 471.

Theresa A. Yugar, Sarah E. Robinson, Lilian Dube, and Teresia Mbari Hinga, eds. *Valuing Lives, Healing Earth: Religion, Gender, and Life on Earth.* ESWTR Studies in Religion Vol. 3. Leuven: Peeters, 2021. 282 pp. €55

Valuing Lives, Healing Earth: Religion, Gender, and Life on Earth, edited by Theresa A. Yugar, Sarah E. Robinson, Lilian Dube, and Teresia Mbari Hinga, explores a wide range of topics in honor of Rosemary Radford Ruether, a formidable ecofeminist theologian and scholar-activist. The book witnesses her life and work and unravels the economic, political, and systemic injustices that support the logic of domination, fervently calling for their deconstruction. Ruether's enthusiasm and commitment to Mother Earth was a testament to her belief and hope that new, different planetary possibilities can improve our world. The authors affirm the relationality shared by all and reflect upon ways of working and supporting the flourishing of the planetary community. The volume helps us re-attune planetary justice, ecological degradation, and animal welfare issues by focusing on how the marginalized are affected by current neo-liberal and capitalist systems.

Aware of their different vulnerabilities, experiences, and contexts, the authors highlight the values of solidarity, friendship, and respect in the ongoing struggle for climate justice. Methodologically, the book applies an intersectional and interrelational lens to climate change, moving us toward a "planetary environmental ethic" that "understands that humans are deeply embedded in evolutionary and ecological processes." Life experiences of women across the globe are contextualized and converge in this volume. The authors develop a collaborative, coalitional vision toward a dynamic, healing, and refreshed earthly existence.

The book consists of eighteen chapters divided into four thematic sections: knowledge, ritual, activism, and food. It provides "a space for conversation across differences and geographies, among people who largely recognize ecological and social justice as life-giving and connected to religious integrity." The first section, on knowledge and methodological approaches, has five chapters. Ivone Gebara opens the section by highlighting black women in Recife, Brazil who collect and sort garbage. This chapter discusses how culture and language are used to demean these women. If they collect garbage/trash, they are seen as garbage themselves, devoid of labor rights, poor, marginalized, and not worthy of a dignified life. In the next chapter, Lillian Dube analyzes the broken status of women due to structural injustices born of colonialism and the sprawling Covid-19 pandemic. Dube raises up a "Virtual Farming Model" that does not solicit "cash handouts," but rather ideological wealth that would "revive the economy, heal the land and restore the dignity of people." In the succeeding chapters, Jea Sophia Oh, Alyssa Moore, and Yuria Celidwen acknowledge human and non-human relationships in our common *oikos*. Indigenous knowledge systems in rituals, symbols, and storytelling that ground people in their context and identity are discussed.

The second section, on rituals, has four chapters. Rebecca Davis interacts with Peruvian women's artwork to show their connection with the land. The new meanings unearthed from the artwork attest to the need for a reflective space for all Earth's inhabitants that will facilitate a "New Creation." In her chapter, "Ecofeminism's Cry," Mary Judith Ress proffers an authentic call and a reminder that we have a common mother, Mother Earth, for whom we have a responsibility to care. Finally, Frédérique Apffel-Marglin calls for external and internal healing of the land, which Sylvia Marcos also supports. This approach shows the centrality of women in indigenous medical practices as an avenue for wholeness and healing within a cosmological worldview.

The third section, on activism, begins with a chapter by Aruna Gnanadason that calls out the industries that contaminate the ecosystem. Gnanadason advocates for an ecofeminist theology that supports an "eco-just" movement and embraces a subjective, relational, and personalized God of compassion. Rosemary Radford Ruether's chapter discusses Wangari Maathai's tree planting movement. The Greenbelt Movement called for peace, access to food, and clean water in a democratic space. Rosalind Hinton discusses the environmental crisis in Louisiana caused by carcinogens created by multinational corporations; she notes that systemic racism and environmentalism are intersectional issues that must both be addressed. Hinton celebrates local women of color's mutuality and solidarity in advocating against corporate polluters. Pamela Brubaker argues that "the cosmovisions of indigenous people are central to their defense of Mother Earth."

The book's final section, on food, opens with Adrienne Krone's chapter advocating for policies and initiatives that contribute positively to the survival of bees and humans. Kelsey Ryan-Simkins and Elaine Nogueira-Godsey then argue for solidarity and justice in food production. They promote food justice that pushes against an industrial food system that exacerbates land depletion. Juan A. Tavárez offers a Mexican model known as *tianguis* that uses ancient ecological culture to heal the Earth. The native *ixtle* (a handbag made of maguey fiber) is one example that could replace the plastic bags that continue to wreak havoc on the environment. Finally, Laurel Marshall Potter's chapter lauds an agroecological indigenous curriculum she witnessed in El Salvador that focuses on community rituals, civic engagement, and food knowledge.

Both the breadth of essays and themes and the variety of authors and contexts contained in this volume should be commended, for it ensures that the book paints an overarching picture of how various groups around the globe are working to conserve Mother Earth. The embrace of Indigenous knowledge systems in earth's conservation highlights a sense of belonging, originality, and attachment that grounds human responsibility to replenish our common home. Varied conceptualizations, symbols, and indigenous rituals around Mother Earth bring forth a mutual concern and need for its sustenance. The authors' realization that feminism is not homogenous is a groundbreaking point of departure for developing feminist philosophies that do not simply respond to patriarchal philosophies but speak to women's lived experiences within their web of relationships. An anthropocosmic approach to all creatures whom Mother Earth sustains is a promising platform for building Earth's healing values.

My one complaint about this volume is that it misses an engagement with One Health, an approach that recognizes that people's health is closely connected to that of animals and our shared environment. Given the recent outbreaks of zoonotic viruses, a chapter on the intersection of gender, ecology, pandemics, and health would have been a valuable addition to this book. Further, the division between the Global North and Global South needs critical unpacking, since it conflates economic and geographic parameters. For instance, it is astonishing that countries like South Africa and Australia, which are in "the South," are not categorized with the rich North due to their financial stability. The demeaning classification is not any different from what Gebara theorizes that the poor (of the Global South) have become: "almost trash to the garbage-producing society that needs them and at the same time refuses them a dignified life." We must address the causes of poverty in "poor" countries. For instance, the deposit of excess carbon emissions in "poor" countries by industrialized countries is an injustice that calls for critical interrogation.

Nevertheless, the book is thought-provoking and teases out diverse methodological approaches to Earth's conservation Undoubtedly, the volume affirms the resilience of women in conserving ecology and it calls upon a human and non-human partnership in this effort of healing the earth. It is, therefore, well worth reading to audiences in all disciplines.

CONTRIBUTORS

Sahir Dewji is an independent researcher and a policy analyst with the government of Canada. He holds a Ph.D. in Religious Studies (WIlfrid Laurier University) and an A.M. in the Histories and Cultures of Muslim Societies (Harvard University). Sahir's area of research focuses primarily on Isamili ethics, identity and practice, cosmopolitan ethics, and religious pluralism. Sahir's broader interests lie in the study of Islam and modernity, including Muslim ethics, social justice, Muslim identity and expressions in the North American context.

Joost Emmerik is a garden and landscape architect. A firm belief in the evoking power of gardens and a need for them in this day and age form the basis of his work. Joost is Head of the Master's program in Landscape Architecture at the Amsterdam Academy of Architecture.

Lucky Issar is an independent researcher and literary scholar. He holds a Ph.D. from Freie Universität Berlin. He has contributed scholarly articles, essays, and book reviews to various publications including Himal, Economic and Political Weekly, Modern Fiction Studies, Victorian Review, and the journal, Literature and Theology.

Michael Kotutwa Johnson is a member of the Hopi Tribe whose research focuses on Indigenous Traditional Ecological Knowledge and Land Use Management schemes related to food, energy, conservation, and water. Michael is also a traditional Hopi dryland farmer. His scholarly works are published in academic peer-reviewed journals as well as featured articles. He currently is an Indigenous Resiliency Specialist with the University of Arizona's School of Natural Resources and the Environment, Cooperative Extension, and the Indigenous Resilience Center.

Nura Sophia Liepsner is a Ph.D. candidate at Princeton University and a research fellow at Princeton's Center for Culture, Society, and Religion. Her scholarship addresses the intersection of knowledge production, interfaith relations, and women's religious authority in modern and early modern Islam. Nura holds a Master of Arts in Religious Studies from Princeton University, a Master of Arts in Near Eastern Languages and Civilizations from Harvard University, and a Bachelor of Arts in Islamic Studies from Free University in Berlin.

Row Light earned their Bachelor's degree in English and Digital/Electronic Media Studies at Scripps College and the Claremont Colleges; they completed a Master's in Theopoetics and Writing at Earlham School of Religion—a degree combining their passion for spirituality and poetry—and have published several poems from their thesis work. Row is a writer and features editor for *The List*. See more at https://www.row-light.com/

Telesia K. Musili is a lecturer at the Department of Philosophy and Religious Studies, University of Nairobi, Kenya. She is also a research fellow at the University of South Africa. Her research interests revolve around the intersection of religion, ethics, media, and environment, focusing on the response to contemporary issues affecting women and society at large.

Meghann Ormond is Associate Professor in Cultural Geography at Wageningen University & Research. Deeply invested in and concerned with how differently mobile people's roots, rights and vulnerabilities are recognized and included in the places they visit and in which they live, her work focuses on how shifting visions and practices of citizenship and belonging impact transnational mobility, heritage, health, and care relationships.

Jon Pahl is the Peter Paul and Elizabeth Hagan Professor at United Lutheran Seminary (Gettysburg/Philadelphia). He also taught formerly at Valparaiso, Temple, and Princeton Universities and earned his Ph.D. at The University of Chicago Divinity School. Jon is the author or editor of seven books, most recently *Fethullah Gülen: A Life of Hizmet—Why a Muslim Scholar in Pennsylvania Matters to the World*, the first critical biography of the controversial and influential Islamic cleric. He was an APRIL summer colloquium fellow in 2003.

Kathryn Reklis is Associate Professor of Modern Protestant Theology and Co-Director of the Comparative Literature program at Fordham University in New York City. Most of her research projects explore different ways Christian theologians and ordinary Christians appeal to beauty, art, and embodied experience as an alternative to the aridity and rationalism they perceive in modernity and asking how those appeals situate Christian theology among supposedly secular modes of knowing and being. She is an avid TV watcher and the Screentime columnist for *The Christian Century*.

Johan Roeland is associate professor in Media, Religion and Popular Culture at the Faculty of Religion & Theology, Vrije Universiteit Amsterdam, and seminary professor at the Remonstrant Brotherhood. His research interests include lived religion and popular culture, religious developments in post-secular contexts, religion and everyday culture, and theology as design.

Irina Sheynfeld is a freelance art historian, painter, and graphic designer. She was born in Odessa, Ukraine where she was trained as a puppet-maker and fine artist. Now, Irina lives and works in New York City with her three sons and a miniature labradoodle, Luke Skywalker.

ERRATA

The editor apologizes for an error made in David Simonowitz's review of Jonathan Homrighausen's book *Planting Letters and Weaving Lines* (73.3, September, 2023, pp. 353-358), The corrected sentences should read as follows:

"Homrighausen remarks that 'Biblical metaphors draw an analogy between touching a tangible object and understanding an intangible idea,' and offers a telling scrip- tural translation: 'Do not ignore the discourse of the aged, . . . from them you grasp [tiqakh] **insight** . . .' I would parse this translation to shed additional light: you grasp **in sight**." (p. 357; corrections in **bold**)

www.ingramcontent.com/pod-product-compliance
Lightning Source LLC
Chambersburg PA
CBHW040300170426
43193CB00020B/2962